JAMES DEAN

PORTRAIT OF COOL

JAMES DEAN

PORTRAIT OF COOL

EDITED BY LEITH ADAMS AND KEITH BURNS

BLAKE

Published by Blake Publishing Ltd,
3, Bramber Court, 2 Bramber Road,
London W14 9PB, England

www.blake.co.uk

This edition published in hardback in 2004

ISBN 1 85782 591 8

British Library Cataloguing-in-Publication Da

A catalogue record for this book is available
from the British Library.

Design by www.envydesign.co.uk

Printed in Singapore by Star Standard

1 3 5 7 9 10 8 6 4 2

Dedication

to James Dean … Star

to Jack L. Warner, Elia Kazan, Nicholas Ray

and George Stevens … Starmakers

FOREWORD

The photographs in this book are reproduced from the original negatives housed in the Warner Bros. Archives at the University of Southern California's School of Cinema-Television. Of the thousands of still photographs taken of Dean during the making of his three starring films, only a limited number were printed and used by the studio for publicity and advertising purposes. The rest lay undisturbed for over three decades until the importance of these images was discovered. But as important as these photographs are, they are made more so by the inclusion of the day-to-day production documents that accompany them.

This book is presented chronologically – film-by-film: *East of Eden*, *Rebel Without a Cause*, and *Giant*. The documents for each film are arranged by relevance, while the photos are arranged as the scenes they represent appear in the film, not by the date on which they were shot. A special section: James Dean: Behind the Camera, follows the photographs from his films. They represent photographs that Dean took himself, on the sets of these films.

Here then, is our celebration of James Dean. He lives on.

Leith Adams, Keith Burns
Los Angeles

CONTENTS

INTRODUCTION

BY DENNIS HOPPER

I'd starred in a television show called *Medic* entitled 'Boy in a Storm'. I played an epileptic. This show aired January 5, 1955. I was 18 years old. Seven studios called my agent wanting to put me under contract. Warner Bros. seemed the most interesting. They told me there was a good chance, since George Stevens had seen the show, of me playing the son of Rock Hudson and Elizabeth Taylor in *Giant*, but that wouldn't shoot for a year. So if Nick Ray would agree to put me in *Rebel Without a Cause*, they would give me a seven year term contract. I had the meeting at Warners with Nick. He said yes, I could be in *Rebel*, and I went under contract.

After being guaranteed that I would be in *Rebel Without a Cause*, I went to see *East of Eden* which was my first experience of seeing James Dean on screen. I thought he was interesting, but imitating Brando. My first vision of Dean was walking with my agent down a hall at Warner Bros., slouching, unshaven, black turtleneck, old Levis, sneakers, thick horn-rimmed glasses, messed hair, skulking head down, sliding by us. My agent whispered, "That's James Dean." I turned around, looked after him and exclaimed in a loud voice, "That's James Dean?"

Later the same day, we went across from Warner Bros. to the drugstore. Jimmy was sitting hunched over a cup of coffee. He was filling his spoon with sugar and, as he dipped it, watching the sugar slowly dissolve into the black coffee, and then filling the spoon and dipping it again, continuing the action over and over and over again. People were talking to him, but he was concentrating only on the spoon and sugar, never responding to their continuous dialogue. He looked not dissimilar to a junkie waiting for his connection on 42nd Street. When my agent introduced me, he didn't turn or even make an audible grunt of recognition.

One of my first jobs, since James Dean was in New York, was to play Jim Stark in the screen test with all of the girls who were tested, everyone from Jayne Mansfield to Natalie Wood. Natalie and I became very close friends, practically inseparable for the next five years. Nick Adams and I moved into a house together. Nicholas Ray and I came close to having a fist fight over Natalie at the chickie run. We were both having affairs with her.

That same night I grabbed James Dean and threw him into a car and told him that I had to know what he was doing as an actor. Because until seeing him I thought I was the greatest young actor in the world, and I didn't understand his method of working. He asked me if I hated my family. I said that yes, I was very angry with them. He said, "Yes, me too. That's our drive to act." I said that when my parents would show up at the theatre I would be very angry, and would feel like saying, "I'm going to show you. I'm going to be somebody." The only thing that was real to them was my becoming a doctor, a lawyer, or an engineer. They felt that pursuing an acting career meant failure. He said he felt the same way when his mother died. He went to her grave and cried, "Mother, why did you leave me?" And that turned into, "Mother, I hate you, I'll show you. I'll be somebody." So our drive has the same beginning, misguided anger and hate, and wanting to communicate through play acting and creating.

James Dean became my personal acting coach, and we went on to do *Giant* together. He told me, "You are technically proficient, you give line readings better than most actors, you study, and you're full of preconceived ideas. You must forget this and learn a new way of working. You must start to do things and not show them. You must not act smoking or drinking a drink, you must simply do it. In the beginning, when you're in front of a camera or on a stage doing these simple realities it will be very difficult, you will be self conscious, but then it will become natural. You must remember you're as real as the people watching, you're real and your audience is real. You must not indicate. You must get rid of all of your preconceived ideas. You must do things, not show things. When someone knocks on the door, you must go and open it, then you see that they have a gun in their hand, and then you react. Simple reality is when you say hello to someone and they say 'Go fuck yourself,' and then you react. But the next time you say 'hello' their response might be a hello with a smile. Your hello must not indicate how you know they are going to respond to you."

Many mornings on *Giant* I would say hello to Jimmy and he wouldn't respond at all, but walk straight on by, deep in concentration.

I have never seen an actor as dedicated, with the extreme concentration and exceptional imagination as James Dean. He could take the written imaginary circumstance and make it his own by improvising — lying on the ground in a fetal position playing with a wound-up toy monkey beating its cymbals, giggling while being searched in the police station because it tickled, standing up in a drunken haze making the sound of sirens with his arms outstretched, hitting his fists into the sergeant's desk, jumping off a diving board into a swimming pool with no water, or doing the voice of Mr. Magoo throughout the movie, which was the voice of Jim Backus, his father in *Rebel* – things that were not written on the page, things that were invented by the actor.

Before starting every scene Jimmy would go off into a corner, holding his head, pacing, doing what at that time was called preparing for a scene or doing his preparation. Then he would tell Nick when he was ready to begin. Later when we were doing *Giant*, I had the opportunity to ask Jimmy what he was doing. Jimmy said most of the time he was trying to clear his mind and approach the scene as if it were for the first time. The most important thing for an actor or an athlete is to be relaxed.

When working with Elizabeth Taylor, in his first scene with her in Texas, there were about a thousand people roped off a hundred yards from the scene. Jimmy walked away in the middle of this first take half way toward the people, pulled out his cock and pissed, and then went back and did the scene. When we were driving back to the hotel that night I said, "Jimmy, I've seen you do a lot of crazy things, but this one I just don't understand." He said, "Well, I was so nervous because of Liz I could barely speak. So I figured if I could go and piss before a thousand people I could go back and do anything in front of the camera."

He had me watch him closely as he grew older and aged in the part of Jett Rink. I remember him being very concerned with the scene he had with Carroll Baker in the bar when he asks her to marry him. Jimmy was 25 playing a 65-year-old man. He had me stand and watch and he would come to me and ask if I believed he was an old man. I told him he looked so old I'm sure an audience would feel that the Carroll Baker character was quite safe because he wouldn't be able to get it up to fuck. He seemed satisfied with that observation, and it was an honest one.

James Dean was the most intense actor and human being I've ever met. People either loved him or hated him. He could eliminate the terms like or dislike or he's OK I never heard them uttered in reference to Jimmy. His idols were Montgomery Clift and Marlon Brando. He said he had Clift in his lowered left hand saying, "Please forgive me," and Brando in his raised right hand saying, "Go fuck yourself," and James Dean was somewhere in the middle.

He said it didn't matter how your lines came out or what crazy kind of behavior you did with your characters. He said you could do Hamlet's soliloquy walking on your hands and eating a carrot as long as the audience could see you and believe you, that your feelings when you are an honest actor show through your eyes.

Jimmy was also very nearsighted. He could barely see four feet in front of him. He thought that it helped him tremendously as an actor because he had to imagine everything that was happening beyond that point. I remember sitting in the commissary at Warner Bros. at a table with Jimmy and Natalie, and Dick Davalos, who played Jimmy's brother in *East of Eden*, came and joined our party. I thought Jimmy was being very rude to Davalos. He didn't say hello and didn't acknowledge his presence. When Dick started having a conversation with Natalie, Jimmy said, "Davalos, is that you?" Dick said, "Yeah, it's me," sarcastically. Jimmy said, "Wow man, it's you," and he got up and hugged him. "I couldn't see you man, I left my glasses in the trailer." I'm not sure whether Davalos, who had been sitting at the table for ten minutes, ever believed him or thought he was just doing a number.

I remember walking outside the commissary at Warners with Jimmy and Jack Warner came up with a major world banker named Mr. Semenenko. Jack Warner had talked his brother Harry into selling Warner Bros. to Semenenko. Semenenko had owned the studio for one week, then Jack had bought it back, screwing his brother out of half ownership of Warner Bros. Mr Warner enthusiastically introduced Mr. Semenenko to Jimmy. Mr. Semenenko reached out his hand to shake hands, and Jimmy reached into his pocket and pulled out a handful of change, threw it at their feet and turned and walked away. I was shocked, not knowing the story, and I just looked at the two men, then turned and followed Jimmy.

I find it unfortunate that the two biographies that have been written about James Dean say that he was gay. James Dean was not gay. The two great loves of his life in Hollywood were Pier Angeli and Ursula Andress. Pier Angeli married Vic Damone. Jimmy sat in the rain on his motorcycle outside the church. She'd asked Jimmy to marry her. He'd asked her to wait until he saw how his career was going. Ursula Andress met John Derek and proceeded to parade him on the set of Giant after Jimmy refused to marry her for the same reason.

Jimmy was not only an internal actor but an expressionist, which came partly from his studying dance. He would physicalise actions, such as the way he lifted himself up on the windmill in *Giant*, or goose-stepped measuring off the land, or his sleight of hand gesture as Jett Rink. He had the amazing capacity to pick up and learn a new trick almost immediately, tossing a rope and making a knot, a card trick from a magician, coin tricks, racing a car.

In my opinion James Dean directed *Rebel Without a Cause*, from blocking all the scenes, setting the cameras, starting the scene, and saying "cut". Nicholas Ray intelligently allowed him to do this.

George Stevens and Jimmy fought from the first day on. Jimmy insisted upon doing long, drawn out behavioural sequences that Stevens knew he would not be able to use in the film. Stevens finally told Jimmy that he should take his little 8mm camera and go out and shoot his own movies, because he was going to make sure that he, Jimmy, was never going to work in Hollywood again. Jimmy was called in before dawn to apply his makeup as an old man in *Giant*. Stevens kept him in his trailer all day and he didn't work. Jimmy told him that night if that ever happened again he would not show up for a day. The next day it happened again. It was on a Friday. Jimmy didn't show up for work on Saturday. Stevens was ready to use him at 7am. The studio went crazy. They couldn't find him all day Saturday, or Sunday, our day off. Monday morning Jimmy was back in makeup. Jack Warner and Steve Trilling (head of production) and George Stevens called Jimmy into Warner's office. They screamed and yelled about the responsibilities of the actor and how much it cost every day whether the cameras rolled or not. The tirade continued for about 20 minutes. The three men fell silent. Jimmy took his feet off the table where he had propped them up and said, "Are you finished, because I want to tell you something. I'm not a fucking machine that you can turn on and off. I come in there every day prepared to do the scenes for that day. Sometimes I've stayed up all night to be tired enough to play this old alcoholic. This time it was one day, the next time it's going to be two days, and then you can start counting the weeks." Not waiting for an answer, he stood up and exited.

A week before Jimmy died he went into a silent order Catholic monastery for three days. Stevens made him promise that he would not race the Porsche Spyder that he had spent his entire *Giant* salary to purchase. I believe it was around $17,000. We weren't finished shooting, but Jimmy had finished principal photography. Later Nick Adams would be asked to dub Dean's voice in the drunk scene in the banquet room of the hotel because Stevens felt his performance was inaudible.

Jimmy came back from the monastery clean shaven, with a haircut, wearing a suit and tie. In the year that I had known Jimmy I'd never seen him personally wear a suit and tie. He came to me and said goodbye. I found this rather curious and later found out that he had said goodbye to a number of people. I would have gone to the race with him, but I had to stay and work. I still found the way he said goodbye bizarre and strange.

My agent asked me to go to the theatre. I was sitting in the audience, waiting for the play to begin. Someone came and got my agent and he went to the lobby. When he came back he said, "I have something to tell you but you must promise me that you won't leave the theatre." By his behaviour and the look on his face I was certain that someone in his family was dead. When he told me that James Dean had died in a car accident, I hit him, muttered the word liar. The lights in the theatre went off and a single spotlight came up on an empty stage. It seemed like an eternity before I ran from the theatre. I thought he must have grandstanded out on one of the turns in the race. I'd seen him go out between cars, hit hay bales and bounce out in front a few times when he won in Palm Springs, right after *Rebel*. I was confused when I heard later that he died in a

simple minded, stupid crash, on the highway, because someone didn't stop at a stop sign.

The notions of James Dean being suicidal are stupid and false. He was given a ticket for going 120mph in a car that would go 180mph, one hour before the crash, but he was only doing 70 mph when a man named Turnipseed ran a stop sign and Jimmy hit him. He lived. Rolf, James Dean's German mechanic, who had been sitting next to Jimmy wearing a seatbelt, lived to become the head mechanic at Mercedes Benz in Germany. Jimmy died. He didn't believe in wearing a seatbelt. He thought it would be better to be thrown free of the machinery.

His death began a series of seances with all of his friends that I've never before or since experienced in my lifetime. Whether in the hysteria of the moment or the youthful pain of the experience, all of us were convinced that we'd had encounters with him.

Elizabeth Taylor came to work on the set everyday. She would start crying hysterically and would have to be sedated. It was three weeks before she was able to complete the last scene for *Giant*.

I'd like to clear up one controversy. Most people remember seeing *Rebel Without a Cause* before Dean died, but Jimmy was only a star to those of us in the industry who knew him in New York and Los Angeles. *East of Eden* was not a commercial success. *Rebel Without a Cause* had not been released yet. Natalie, Nick and I went out and promoted it throughout the country. After its tremendous success, *East of Eden* was re-released to become a commercial success and then *Giant*.

Every time I go to Europe I remember that James Dean never saw Europe, but yet I see his face everywhere. There's James Dean, Humphrey Bogart and Marilyn Monroe – windows of the Champs Élyseés, discos in the south of Spain, restaurants in Sweden, t-shirts in Moscow.

My life was confused and disoriented by his passing. My sense of destiny destroyed – the great films he would have directed, the great performances he would have given, the great humanitarian he would have become, and yet, he's the greatest actor and star I have ever known.

"Paul Osborn, who was writing the screenplay (*East of Eden*), said I should have a look at the young man playing the bit part of an Arab in a play at the John Golden Theatre. I wasn't impressed with James Dean – I'd begun to think about Brando again – but to please Osborn I called Jimmy into Warners' New York offices, for a closer look. When I walked in he was slouched at the end of a leather sofa in the waiting room, a heap of twisted legs and rags, looking resentful for no particular reason. I didn't like the expression on his face, so I kept him waiting. I also wanted to see how he'd react to that. It seemed that I'd out-roughed him, because when I called him into my office, he'd dropped the belligerent pose. We tried to talk, but conversation was not his gift, so we sat looking at each other. He asked me if I wanted to ride on the back of his motorbike. I didn't enjoy the ride. He was showing off – a country boy not impressed with big-city traffic. When I got back to the office, I called Paul and told him this kid actually was Cal in *East of Eden*; no sense looking further or 'reading' him. I sent Dan to see Steinbeck ... John thought Dean a snooty kid. I said that was irrelevant; wasn't he Cal? John said he sure as hell was, and that was it."

ELIA KAZAN

(*Elia Kazan: A Life*   Alfred A. Knopf   New York   1988)

MOTION PICTURE ASSOCIATION
OF AMERICA, INC.
8480 BEVERLY BOULEVARD
HOLLYWOOD 48, CALIFORNIA
WEBSTER 3-7101

ERIC JOHNSTON
PRESIDENT

JOSEPH I. BREEN
VICE PRESIDENT AND
DIRECTOR
PRODUCTION CODE ADMINISTRATION

December 2, 1953

Mr. J.L. Warner
Warner Bros. Pictures, Inc.
4000 W. Olive Avenue
Burbank, California

Dear Mr. Warner:

This goes to you in confirmation of our conference yesterday with Messrs. Steve Trilling, Finlay McDermid and Walter MacEwen with regard to the first draft script of the Steinbeck novel, EAST OF EDEN. The purpose of the conference was to discuss the fact that the present script contains material which could not be approved under the requirements of the Production Code.

This unacceptable material has to do with the various scenes laid in a brothel. As we explained in some detail, it has been the steadfast procedure of the Code Administration not to approve scenes dealing with any of the mechanics of prostitution. This would include scenes laid in or around brothels.

This procedure of ours was given official sanction by the Board of Directors of the Association in the case of our rejection of the Italian picture THE BICYCLE THIEF, which contained a scene laid in a brothel. Our contention that this type of material was not suitable for the mixed family audiences to which our pictures appeal was unanimously sustained by the Board.

When we discussed this story previously with Mr. Trilling and Mr. McDermid and Mr. Kazan about a year ago, we agreed that it would be acceptable to establish the fact that Adam's wife had become a prostitute. But we endeavored to make it clear at that time that we did not feel that we could go any further than merely establishing the fact, which is necessary to bring about

cc Trilling

Warner - Page 2

December 2, 1953

the climactic tragedy of the story. At the conference yesterday, we discussed certain tentative ideas as to how this objective could be attained and still steer clear of any unacceptable exploitation of brothels or prostitution.

Whenever you feel it advisable to discuss this matter any further, we should be happy to place ourselves at your convenience.

There is one other element in the script which is also unacceptable. This arises from the attitude of the Sheriff and possibly others in the town, who seem to condone the existence of the brothel, merely because it is well managed and orderly. Naturally, under the requirements of the Code, we could not approve any dialogue which seemed to condone or justify organized prostitution.

Cordially yours,

Joseph I. Breen

KAZAN

McDERMID

Dear Gadge!

As you suggested, I called the Breen Office and being unable to reach Shurlock talked instead to Vizzard. I asked him whether he could see any objection to showing the opening as it now stands with Kate walking along a disreputable street and Cal following her looking at the "houses" as he goes -- if the place Kate finally entered was not a house but a saloon and our further interiors would take place in the saloon. Vizzard could see no objection.

I further asked if we could establish that Kate owned not only the saloon but a house - or houses and that the saloon was a so__ of a front. Vizzard agreed that this would be a possible treat__ depending on how the actual scene was written and filmed. He cautioned against showing any actual solicitation or more obvi__ details, but he did accept the general idea.

I read the Ann scene to him and almost all of it would play - __ minor line changes.

__cifically!   April 27, 1954   Page 28.   "This your first time"?

"This is Kate's place"
(suggested alternative)
"We all work for Kate".

Page 30.   "This is a tough house".
"(This is a tough place)!"

MEMO FOR THE FILES

Re: EAST OF EDEN - Warner Bros.

This morning Mr. Shurlock, Mr. Dougherty and Mr. Vizzard met with Elia Kazan, Finlay McDermid and Walter McEwen at Warner Brothers Studio to discuss the estimating script, received in this office on April 19, 1954, for this property.

The second problem has to do with the indication that our two romantic leads indulge in an illicit sex relationship as we come near the climax of the story. The specific problem with this sex affair consists in the fact that the girl gives herself to the boy as an act of compassion, to lift him out of his agony after having been rejected for the final time by his father. this seems to give illicit sex a kind of therapeutic dimension, as well as to make it seem an act of kindness and humanity. the __erivative of this is that it seems to be thoroughly justified.

__ replied that he would explore ways and __ __f the b___
__ss___

__R BROS. PICTURES, INC.
BURBANK, CALIFORNIA

TRILLING

MR. McDERMID

Dear Steve!

I was in the throes of writing you a routine report of Friday evenings Breen Office meeting on EAST OF EDEN when I had a phone call from Shurlock which complicates the report somewhat. On Friday evening they okayed the line "Is there a law against following the town madam?". This morning they rechecked the list of forbidden words and found that "madam" is one of them. "prostitute" is not on the list. Only way in which we could secure use of the word "madam" would be to go to the Board of Directors. I don't know whether the term is sufficiently well known, but one synonym for madam is Queen Bee.

Shurlock first broached the point in the meeting and then reinforced it over the telephone that he would like to have a discussion with you, me and/or Mort Blumenstock about the proposed advertising and exploitation on the picture so that emphasis is not placed __ the __er on the sensational aspects of the story. In short, the Breen boys are a little frightened by their own temerity and need to be reassured by you and Mort. It is true, as Gadge __ it, "We are still getting away with murder"

Briefly, we will

Dear Jack: Just a note to say goodbye and to thank you for
Your understanding. The WATERFRONT movie did take a lot
longer than I figured - or than you likely figured. But
you never sowacked (how the hell do you spell that word??)
about the delay. I appreciate. I leave by boat tomorrow
and will be ready to go to work in real earnest in four weeks.
I'll come right out there and stay.

About casting. I think Dean is o.k. Impress on him or
have some one impress on him again when he arrives out there,
the great importance of living an outdoor life,sunshine
exercise food and fucking. Just all the healthy things,and
lots of sleep. He's an odd kid and I think we should make
him as handsome as possible.

I consider the kid:Dick Davlos a fair
possibility for Aron. I'm not nuts about him,but there is
something nice about him and perhaps he can do it. I think
Solly should immediately start looking out there to match
Dean. There was a kid in California I once used as a child
Thespian: Darryl Kickman. But I think a more possible field
would be the little theatres,college theatres etc. Now that
we have Dean we can match him. Dick Davlos isn't going to
run away,and if we cant do better we can always use him.

About Abra. Julie Harris is a brilliant actress. She is
very possibly too old. A friend of mine Gjon Mili (the
famous Life Photographer) is doing a test of her and Dean,
photographic only,this coming week. He is a sensitive person
and if he cant make Dean and Julie Harris match no one can.
But I dont in any case want Abra to look older than Cal.
Of the three girls I tested in New York I like Joanne Woodward
best. She is in the possible but not enthusiastic quality.

Kate could be KAY MEDFORD. a brilliant new actress in
New York. I advised Harry Mayer to "put a string on her".
But you might have some one remind him again.

For the old man I'm still interested in getting an
old western star. But,what about Gary Cooper? He has been
quoted as saying that he'd do anything I wanted to do with
him. Most of that kind of talk is strictly for the cocktail
hour. But Cooper seems like a very sincere guy. I'd like to
have him very much and could even build the part up a little
- a little,only a little - for him. Then there is Freddie
March. I'd rather have an outdoor type.

I'd still like Harry Stradling,but they tell me he's
gone to Rome for a long time. Could Steve check on this.
Second choice: Russ Metty. Jim Wong Howe. I don't want
Sam Leavitt

I still dont know whether I'm going to do it part on
location or what? First thing I do after I check in and check
a few things is to take the night train to Salinas and
look around up there a couple of days. John Steinbeck told me
where there were some old streets.

I think the whole script needs about forty pages taken
out of it,and moved outdoors more etc. But that can all wait.

[handwritten in left margin:] mail me Your reactions to N.Y. City

[handwritten in right margin:] free!

March 10th, 1954

Dear Gadg:

Thanks for your letter. I sympathize with
your trials and tribulations on WATERFRONT.
However, now that it is behind you, with
the rest you are going to get you will come
out "fit as a fiddle and ready for love".

About the boy, Dean, inasmuch as your
impression of him is a good one, we
naturally will go along with you. You said
he is an odd kid. I hope he isn't too odd
as it is getting to the point now that when
we make pictures with odd people, the whole
machine is thrown out of order. You know
it only takes one odd spark plug to make the
motor miss. I, too, am fed up with people
who are too odd. That doesn't mean Marlon
Brando is odd. I am sure he knows the score
and just makes everything tough in order to
make himself different. However, the hell
with Brando. He was in a picture called,
THE WILD ONE and even the operators refused
to stay in the booth. As our good pal, Billy
Shakespeare said virtually 500 years ago,
"The Play is Still the Thing".

Solly Baiano and Bill Orr are going to work
on the casting problem. Julie Harris is a
great talent and we are anxiously awaiting
the Gjon Mili test. Re: the cameraman, we will
end up with someone you like and who has ability.
I like your idea of going to Salinas as soon as
you get here. However, I like your idea best
that the script needs to be boiled down and
forty pages taken out. Right now, I will settle
for thirty-five. Every good wish from Steve and
the gang.

                              Sincerely,

Mr. E. Kazan
167 E. 74th St.
New York, New York

WESTERN UNION

W. P. MARSHALL, PRESIDENT

FX-1201

SYMBOLS
DL=Day Letter
NL=Night Letter
LT=Int'l Letter Telegram
VLT=Int'l Victory Ltr.

WG-14. I NEW YORK NY, FEB. 5, 1954.

KAZAN (VIA MAYER) TO JL ------. FOUND NEW BOY THAT I MOST ENTHUS-
TIC ABOUT AND WHO, COULD MAKE PICTURE THIS SPRING SO WE DONT HAVE
WAIT. UNTIL JUNE. ALSO HAVE GIRL I LIKE AND WILL TEST BOTH OF THEM
FROM TUESDAY.

THE COMPANY WILL APPRECIATE SUGGESTIONS FROM ITS PATRONS CONC

WESTERN UNION

W. P. MARSHALL, PRESIDENT

FX-1201

SYMBOLS
DL=Day Letter
NL=Night Letter
LT=Int'l Letter Telegram
VLT=Int'l Victory Ltr.

CLASS OF SERVICE

This is a full-rate
Telegram or Cable-
gram unless its de-
ferred character is in-
dicated by a suitable
symbol above or pre-
ceding the address.

WG-1. I NEW YORK NY FEB. 8, 1954.

MAYER TO TRILLING AND ORR ------ KAZAN DESIRES SEE TEST FILM JIMMY
DEAN LEE PHILLIPS. ALSO TEST LUCY ANN MCALEER WITH KARL MALDEN. PLEASE
AIR EXPRESS SOON AS POSSIBLE.

DEAN & PHILLIPS. TEST Now Rm #5
McLORDS OFFICE TRYING LOCATE

WESTERN UNION

W. P. MARSHALL, PRESIDENT

FX-1201

SYMBOLS
DL=Day Letter
NL=Night Letter
LT=Int'l Letter Telegram
VLT=Int'l Victory Ltr.

CLASS OF SERVICE

This is a full-rate
Telegram or Cable-
gram unless its de-
ferred character is in-
dicated by a suitable
symbol above or pre-
ceding the address.

WG-2. NEW YORK NY FEB. 11, 1954.

KAZAN (VIA MAYER) TO JL (CONFIDENTIAL) ------ DEAR JACK: DID NOT
HAVE GOOD REACTION WILLIAMS SCRIPT BUT WILL STUDY AGAIN THIS WEEKEND
AND CALL YOU FIRST OF WEEK. THINK I FOUND RIGHT BOY FOR EDEN AND
TESTING TUESDAY. THRU CUTTING WATERFRONT END NEXT WEEK BUT FIRST WANT
TAKE VACATION AND AFTER THAT WILL GO WORK AGAIN. THOROUGHLY TIRED
RIGHT NOW. BEST.

CONCERNING ITS SERVICE

"The discovery of James Dean by Elia Kazan and Warner Bros. is reflected in these telegrams from Steve Trilling's files: the Jack L. Warner Collection, USC Cinema-Television Library. Trilling, Executive Assistant to Jack Warner, for his own personal reference, would 'Line Out' and initial each piece of correspondence that crossed his desk, indicating he'd handled the matter."

	WARNER BROS.	50%
	Pictures Present	5%
Must be 50% size of title in adv.	John Steinbeck's	50%
	"EAST OF EDEN"	100%
Must be 50% size of title in adv.	An Elia Kazan Production	50%
	Starring	
Must star on scr. & in adv. preceding Dean.	JULIE HARRIS	50%
No adv. obligation	JAMES DEAN	50%
Star on scr. & in adv.	RAYMOND MASSEY	50%
	with	
Must be in adv.	BURL IVES	25%
	RICHARD DAVALOS	25%
	JO VAN FLEET	25%
No adv. obligation.	ALBERT DEKKER	25%
	LOIS SMITH	25%
	HAROLD GORDON	10%
	LONNY CHAPMAN	10%
	in CinemaScope	50%
	in WarnerColor	50%
	Print by TECHNICOLOR	15%
No adv. obligation. use where and when space permits.	Music by Leonard Rosenman	3%
NOTE: Where possible, increase to 30%.	Screen Play by Paul Osborn	30%
	Directed by Elia Kazan	40%
	A Warner Bros. Picture	5%
	* * *	
	(AS O.K.'D BY J.L.WARNER)	

FOURTH
REVISED
TRADE AD.
BILLING

"EAST OF EDEN"

Elia Kazan   #810

STAFF & CAST

STAFF

Producer-Director	Elia Kazan	Ext. 771
Unit Manager	Don Page - 4355 Clybourn	Su 2-3150
Asst. Director	Horace Hough - 11633 La Maida St.	Po 6-3546
2nd Asst. "	Carter Gibson - 10955 Bluffside	Su 2-9041
3rd " "	Claude Archer - 4541 Talofa - N.H	Su 2-1354
Art Director	James Basevi - 456 Skyewiay	Ariz 7-5087
" "	Mal Bert - 436 E. Fairview Blvd.- Inglewood	Or 8-1446
Cutter	Owen Marks - 5013 Ventura Blvd.	St 4-3440
Cameraman	Ted McCord - 965 Verdugo Circle	Ci 3-6269
Operator	Andy Anderson - 4120 Brunswick	No 3-0372
Camera Asst.	Fred Terso - 5808 Willowcrest Ave.	Su 1-7972
Co-ordo.	John Hambleton - 8105 N. Wilcox - Holly.	Ho 4-5151
Camera Asst.	Wm. J. Ranaldi - 5523 Fulton - Van Nuys	St 5-5110
Script Sup.	Irva Mae Ross - 131 So. Avon -Burbank Idyllwild	Th 2-8955 8-0722
Dial. Dir.	Guy Thomajan	
Stillman	Jack Albin - 846 N. Fairfax	Ho 4-0255
Gaffer	Charles O'Bannon - 2701 Laurel Canyon	Ho 3-8324
Best Boy	Ernest Long - 1115 N. Avon St.	Th 6-1638
Grip	William Classen-3553 Rosemary St.(Glendale)	Ch 9-1038
Set Dresser	Bill Wallace - 3100 Clark St.	Th 6-2959
Prop Man	Red Turner - 3734 S. Norton Ave.	Ax 4-8479
Asst. Prop Man	George Sweeney - 4039 LaSalle St.	Ve 8-4685
Mixer	Stanley Jones - 4536 Arcola Ave.	Su 1-3754
Recorder	Ed McDonald - 3322 Charleston Way	Ho 4-5217
Boom Boy	Everet Hughes - 17190 Lassen St.	Di 3-4085
Wardrobe Man	Leon Roberts - 7570½ DeLongpre	Ho 5-0011
" Woman	Ora Johnson - 6314 Morella	Su 3-5792
Hairdresser	Tillie Starriet - 5446 Woodman	St 5-4494
Makeup Man	Robert Ewing - 11912 Riverside Dr.	Su 2-8763
Secretary-to	Rhea Burakoff - 8241 DeLongpre	Ho 5-2585
Mr. Kazan		Ext. 771

CAST

"Adam"	Raymond Massey	
"Abra"	Julie Harris - 3300 Riverside Dr.	Th 8-3075
"Cal Trask"	James Dean - 3908 W. Olive - Apt. 3	Th 2-5752 Ariz 8-2018
"Aaron Trask"	Dick Davalos - " " " " "	Th 2-5752
"Kate"	Jo VanFleet - 3300 Riverside Dr.	Th 2-5892
"Will	Albert Dekker - 240 Bently Circle	Ariz 9-6758
"Ann"	Lois Smith-3401 W. Olive (Studio Motel)-	Th 6-6940
"Rantani"	Nick Dennis- 1030½ Cory Ave.	Cr 4-3962
"Joe"	Timothy Carey - 148 E. 75th St.	Cr 5-7203
	(Carlos Dvarado)	
"Sam"	Berle Ives - Bev. Wilshire Hotel	
"Mr. Albrecht"	Harold Gordon	
"Roy"	Lonnie Chapman	
"Piscora"		

E. G. STACEY

James Dean and Julie Harris pose for pre-production wardrobe tests for the first scenes of *East of Eden*. Note that the dark

sweater and shoes Dean wears in this test were changed for lighter coloured articles in the actual film.

A less than enthusiastic James Dean (Cal Trask) and a hidden Richard
Davalos (as his brother Aron) pose with Jo Van Fleet's costume.
The camera assistant blocking Davalos holds a colour chart which was
used as a reference when printing the film.

On the backlot of Warner Bros. Studio in Burbank, California, the publicity department posed James Dean for a

series of now legendary photographs to announce their new star. A shot of Dean's head, surrounded by a swirl of fencewire,

is one of the most famous. This is how it was done.

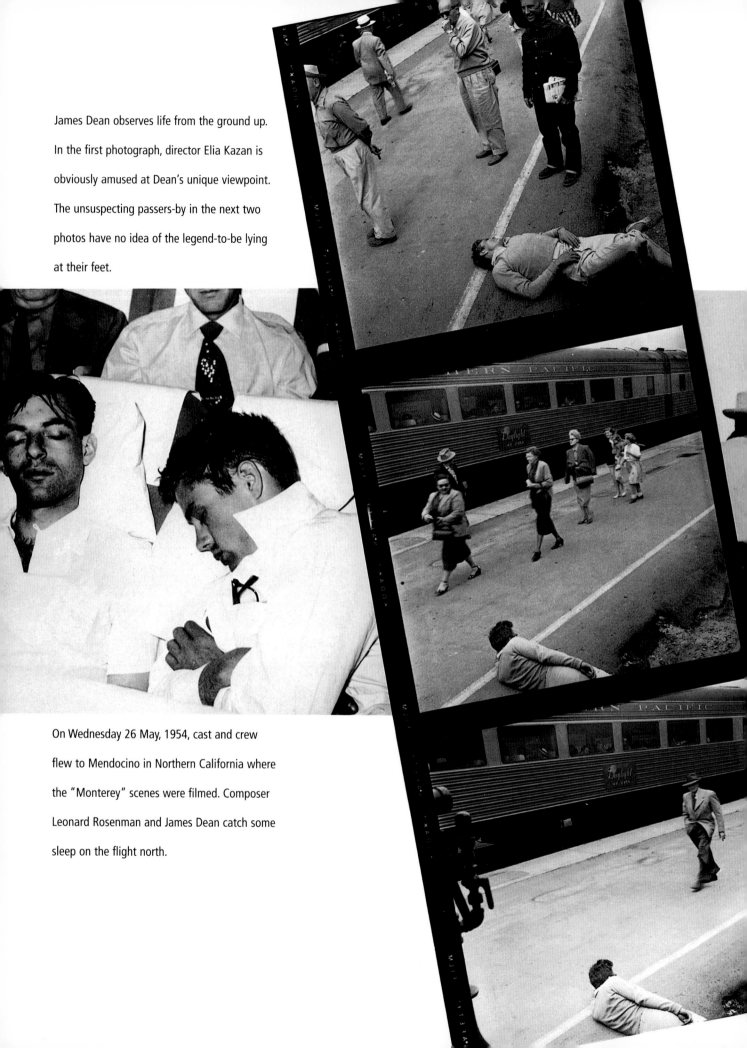

James Dean observes life from the ground up. In the first photograph, director Elia Kazan is obviously amused at Dean's unique viewpoint. The unsuspecting passers-by in the next two photos have no idea of the legend-to-be lying at their feet.

On Wednesday 26 May, 1954, cast and crew flew to Mendocino in Northern California where the "Monterey" scenes were filmed. Composer Leonard Rosenman and James Dean catch some sleep on the flight north.

"I really loved him. And I really loved
working with him. It was a unique
experience in my life. I never worked with
an actor again that was quite that way."
JULIE HARRIS

Cinematographer Ted McCord
checks the quality of light for
James Dean in Mendocino.

James Dean and Timothy Carey (Joe) work out their confrontation scene in front of Kate's "house" ...

JOE: "Now look, why're you followin' Kate around? What's the idea, squirt?"

Between takes, James Dean looks …

leaps …

launches …

lounges ...

James Dean in the ice house.

"Dean couldn't budge the huge block of ice until Elia Kazan made a derogatory remark about Dean's acting ability.

The trick worked. Dean was so incensed that in a fit of anger he picked up the ice and threw it to the ground below."

WARNER BROS. PUBLICITY RELEASE TED ASHTON: 6/23/54

Looking down on the "bible-reading" scene as Elia Kazan (top) rehearses Raymond Massey (left) and James Dean (right) in their parts as righteous father and rebellious son.

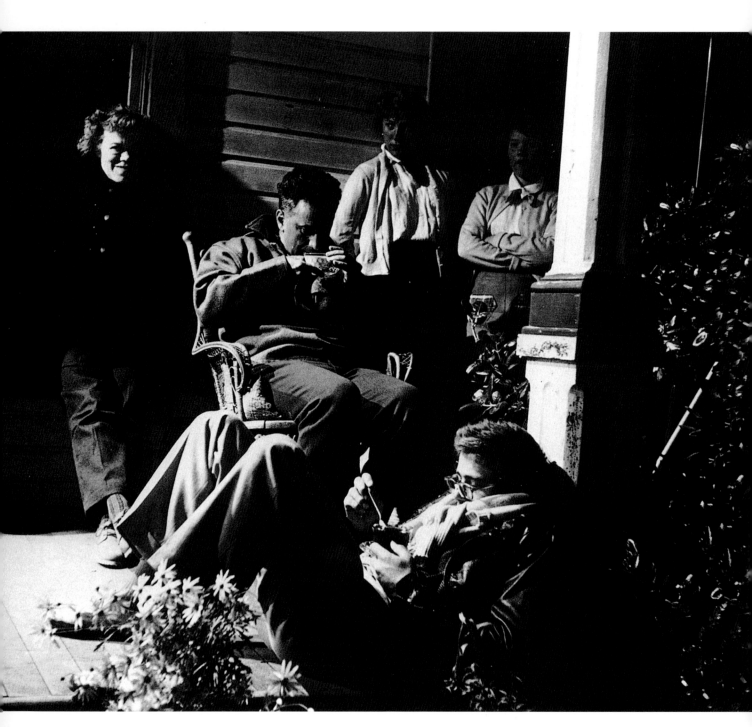

On a chilly night in Mendocino, Elia Kazan and

James Dean sip hot drinks and try to stay warm on

the front porch of Kate's "house".

Burl Ives – as the understanding sheriff of Monterey –

consoles James Dean's troubled Cal, giving him advice

about the mother who left him so long ago.

James Dean and Lydia Guerero await direction from Elia Kazan beside the railroad tracks outside Salinas, California.

James Dean, back in action following his discussion with Kazan, finds another able conversationalist in actor-friend Nick Dennis who plays Rantani, the bean farmer.

"Kazan insisted that Dean climb a rope, race around the gym and then run downstairs into the scene in the locker room. Unfortunately, the youthful Dean was in such good condition that he had to negotiate six round trips before he was sufficiently breathless to meet Kazan's requirements."

WARNER BROS. PUBLICITY RELEASE TED ASHTON: 6/4/54

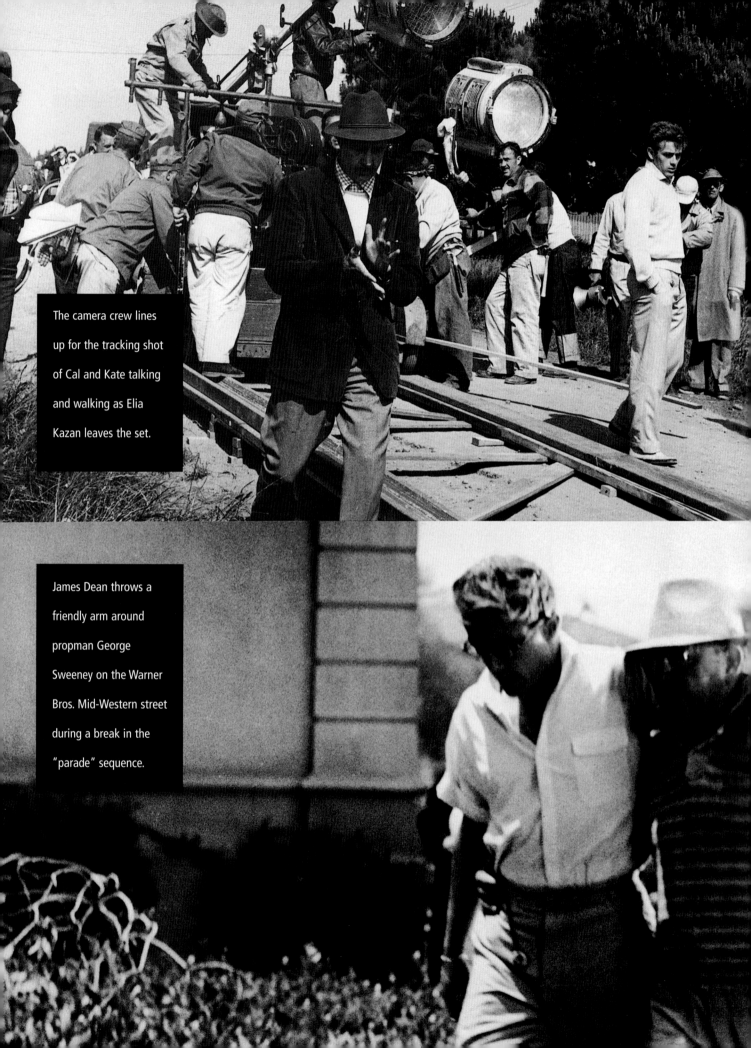

The camera crew lines up for the tracking shot of Cal and Kate talking and walking as Elia Kazan leaves the set.

James Dean throws a friendly arm around propman George Sweeney on the Warner Bros. Mid-Western street during a break in the "parade" sequence.

Waiting for the parade to begin … James Dean and kids.

"Then Jimmy bought a motorbike … I told him I didn't want to chance an accident, and that he absolutely couldn't ride the bike until the film was over."

ELIA KAZAN

Elia Kazan lines up a shot of James Dean watching his crop grow as cinematographer Ted McCord looks on.

James Dean … rings the bell.

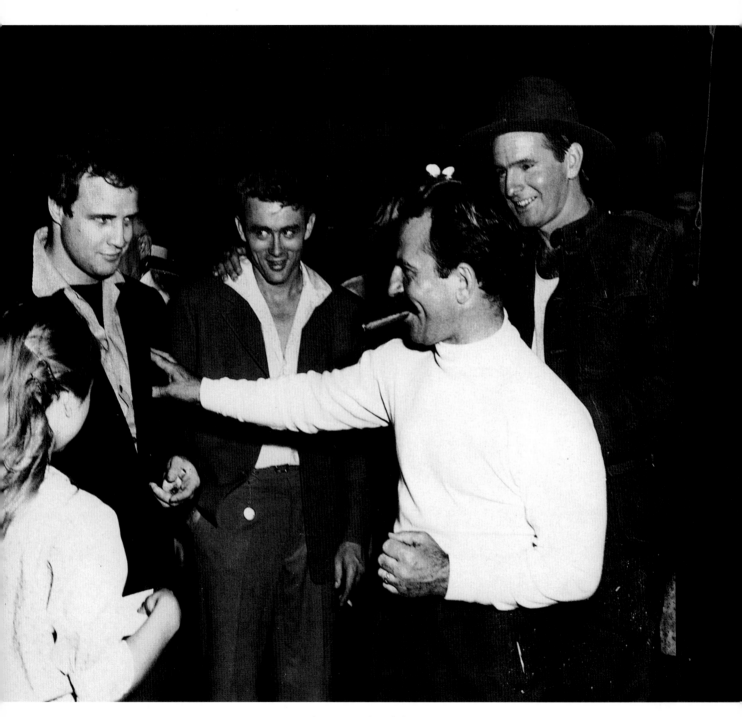

Nick Dennis picks a fight …

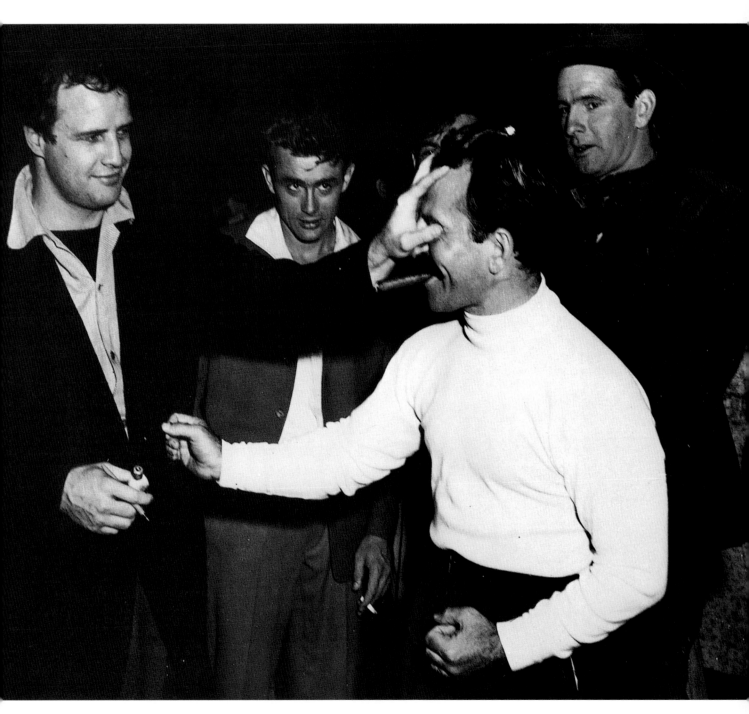

… with the wrong actor. Note the changes in expression of James Dean and the "soldier" as an immobile

Marlon Brando grabs Nick Dennis by the face.

As James Dean looks on, Elia Kazan instructs an elderly extra for her motion picture debut on the carnival set.

"As I look around, I see a complete carnival set-up: a huge ferris wheel, a merry-go-round, a shooting gallery, a side-show, various games of chance and stalls with candied apples, salt water taffee, and soft drinks."

WARNER BROS. PUBLICITY RELEASE

TED ASHTON 7/27/54

"I doubt that Jimmy would ever have got through *East of Eden* except for an angel on our set. Her name was Julie Harris,

and she was goodness itself with Dean, kind and patient and everlastingly sympathetic."

ELIA KAZAN

To everyone's amusement, James Dean tries to light his cigar on a ferris wheel lightbulb.

… Roll!

"I came to Hollywood to act,

not to charm society. The

objective artist has always

been misunderstood."

JAMES DEAN WARNER BROS.

PUBLICITY RELEASE

CARL COMBS: 3/9/55

"So Gadge (Kazan) endured the slouchings, the

eye-poppings, the mutterings and all the wilful

eccentricities … he said to me one morning …

'Bear with me, Ray, I'm getting solid gold!'"

RAYMOND MASSEY

Richard Davalos (foreground), Julie Harris and
James Dean (background) await Raymond
Massey's entrance into the house for the
famous "birthday party" scene.

"I couldn't remember ever having seen a young man with such power, so many facets of expression, so much sheer invention as this actor."

HEDDA HOPPER

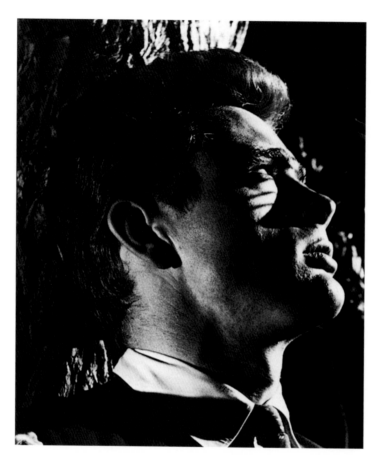

"Acting is the most logical way for people's

neuroses to express themselves."

JAMES DEAN

A jealous Aron (Richard Davalos) "pulls" Abra (Julie Harris) away from Cal (James Dean) in the backyard of the Trask home on stage 6 at Warner Bros. studio.

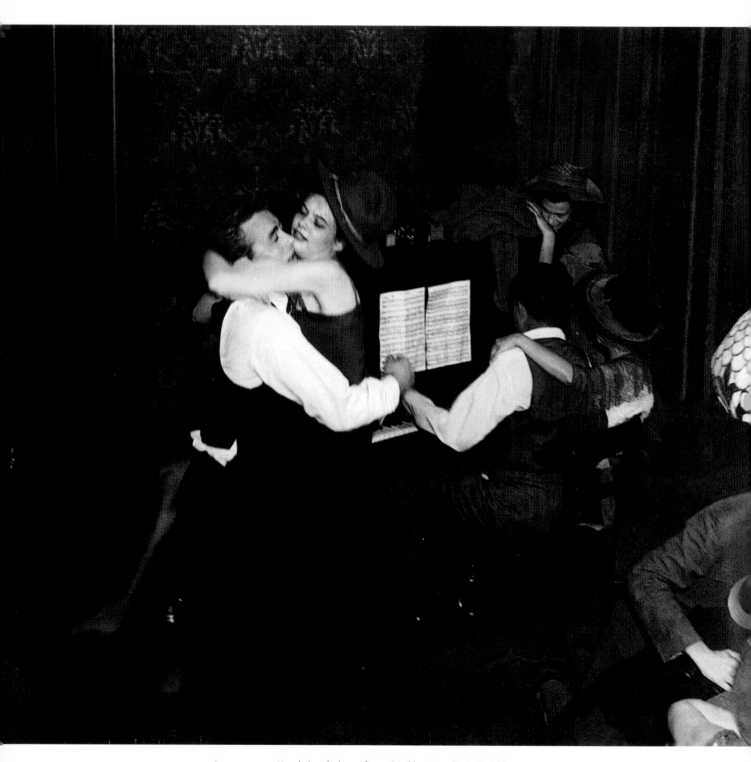

In a scene at Kate's brothel, cut from the film, Ann (Lois Smith)

wraps her legs around Cal (James Dean) just after he has

"introduced" Aron to their mother (Jo Van Fleet).

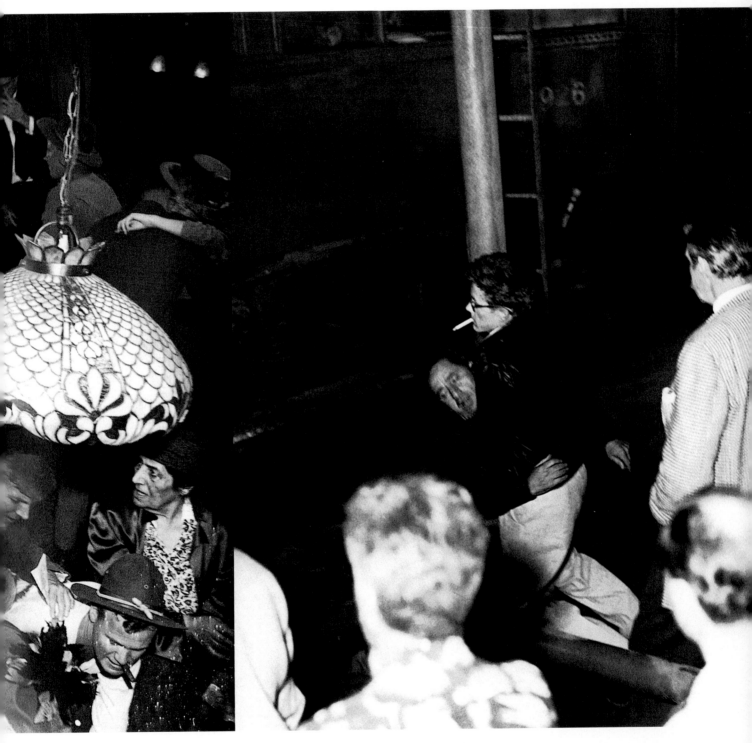

In a rehearsal for the climax of the film,

Elia Kazan shows Raymond Massey how to collapse

from a stroke into James Dean's arms.

WESTERN UNION

W. P. MARSHALL, PRESIDENT

SYMBOLS
DL=Day Letter
NL=Night Letter
LT=Int'l Letter Telegram
VLT=Int'l Victory Ltr.

1220

NEW YORK NY MARCH 10, 1955.

JL TO TRILLING AND BLUMENSTOCK ------ OPENING OF EAST OF EDEN

SCRIBE THIS AMAZING PICTURE.] JL-TRILLING-BLUMENSTOCK

TREMENDOUS. REVIEWS EXCELLENT. AUDIENCE ENTHRALLED. HARD TO FIND WORDS

SCHNEIDER TO JL ------ BATTLE CRY WEDNESDAY PARAMOUNT NEW YORK

NEW YORK CONFIDENTIAL VICTORIA 1556] JL-TRILLING-BLUMENSTOCK

NORTON TO MUELLER ------ YOUR WIRE RECEIVED WILL TAKE PROMPT

ION TO SECURE PROPER EQUIPMENT AND COMPLETE COOPERATION FOR GRAHAM.

GARDS.] MUELLER

26, 1955

Mr. Elia Kazan,
Forrest Theater,
Philadelphia, Pa.

Dear Gadge:

Harry Mayer sent me the reviews and has told me now
derfully well the show was received in Philly...appar
another big, big smash for you when it arrives in New
York.

Equally as good news is the excellent reception EDEN
been receiving in these few early release dates -- cri
cally as well as commercially. I thought this week's
magazine review was unusually good, if you will overlo
some of its snide asides. Opened today LA Egyptian and
Paramount Downtown and at 4:00PM the figures were as
strong as BATTLE CRY -- our biggest grossing picture in
years and years. You always knew EDEN had quality but
were concerned about it being "box office"; obviously n
it's all of that.

That's all, know you are up to your neck in work and
sweat...keep making them good in all directions.

Love from the bunch.

As ever,

Steve Trilling

PS

Mort Blumenstock said he would forward you a set of
the local reviews first thing tomorrow.

Michael Todd Company, Inc.

WESTERN UNION
INTERNATIONAL COMMUNICATIONS
CABLEGRAM

W. P. MARSHALL, PRESIDENT

TO OBTAIN FAST AND
ACCURATE SERVICE
INSERT
Via W.U.Cables

Feb. 10 1955

1256 (7/50)

CHECK

ACCOUNTING INFORMATION

TIME FILED

Mr. Elia Kazan
187 East 74th St. NYC   Via

ar Gadge:

This is a fan letter. I saw East of Eden last night and after I recovered from the impact and
was walking away from the projection room, I attempted to analyze why I was so spellbound.
Most audiences don't do that. They just react to a picture good or bad and let it go at that
and want no reasons. But not so with me. I had to find out why I was so moved. First,
the direction and casting call for new adjectives. The use of the camera results in not a whole
best use of Cinemascope to date or for many dates to come. The composition will give you
new method and technique for Cinemascope. I think that 20th Century Fox should come of
a substantial piece of their company for what you have done to make Cinemascope and passed the
age. As I was still under the spell of the picture I was walking up Broadway and the name,
itor Theatre and saw the billing for East of Eden and noticed the words around the marquee,
city that the arner masterminds are attempting to deprive the public of finding and making
this star themselves. And being the presumptuous guy I am, special star coming up. I thought what a
wire to Jack Warner. I don't feel that anything could stop this guy Dean from being a star
although such pre-labels have stopped other potentials. In this case I don't think this could
happen, but it is too bad to spoil the unconscious genius's, the public's fun. When

---

UNION
COMMUNICATIONS
GRAM

W. P. MARSHALL, PRESIDENT

ions, rules and regulations of The Western Union Telegraph Company set forth in its tariffs on file with the Federal Communications Commission:

TO OBTAIN FAST AND
ACCURATE SERVICE
INSERT
Via W.U.Cables

19

1256 (7/50)

CHECK

ACCOUNTING INFORMATION

TIME FILED

10   Elia Kazan (continued)   Via

Jack Warner receives this copy from me he will not only think I am presumptuous
but he will know that I am not a constant knocker because I had breakfast with him the
morning after A Star is Born premiere and in the face of the tremendous build-up and
notices, I not only was not overwhelmed, I was somewhat pessimistic. And this
morning I wish I had the power of description to really show my enthusiasm for a
project of which I have no direct interest except that I am proud to be associated
with the business that made East of Eden, show business and to quote our songwriter
friend, of which there is no business like.

Regards,

Mike

cc Mr. Jack Warner

WESTERN UNION

CLASS OF SERVICE

This is a full-rate Telegram or Cablegram unless its deferred character is indicated by a suitable symbol above or preceding the address.

W. P. MARSHALL, PRESIDENT

FX-1201

SYMBOLS

DL=Day Letter
NL=Night Letter
LT=Int'l Letter Telegram
VLT=Int'l Victory Ltr.

The filing time shown in the date line on telegrams and day letters is STANDARD TIME at point of origin. Time of receipt is STANDARD TIME at point of destination

WG-3. I NEW YORK NY FEBRUARY 11. 1955.

COLOE TO BLUMENSTOCK ------ RE DEAN. HE HAS BEEN ABSOLUTELY IMPOSSIBLE. HAS BEEN EXTREMELY UNCOOPERATIVE AND REFUSED TO SEE FINE LINEUP OF NEWSPAPER INTERVIEWS WE HAD SET FOR HIM. FINALLY CONVINCED HIM TO SIT FOR INTERVIEWS WHEREUPON HE FOULED HIMSELF UP AND GOT ONE MAGAZINE WRITER SORE AS BLAZES. HAVE ASKED KAZAN GIVE US ASSIST AND CONFIDENTIALLY GADGE SAYS HE DOESN'T WANT TO BE FATHER CONFESSOR TO THIS KID. COULD HAVE USED DEAN TO GREAT ADVANTAGE FOR EDEN BUT WAY HE IS ACTING HE CAN DO US MORE HARM THAN GOOD. HE NEEDS GOOD SCRUBBING BEHIND EARS.

THE COMPANY WILL APPRECIATE SUGGESTIONS FROM ITS PATRONS CONCERNING ITS SERVICE

"The excitement with which *East of Eden* and James Dean were received pleased Warner Bros. immensely and even this telegram (above) to publicity head Mort Blumenstock detailing Dean's difficulties in meeting the press could not dampen their enthusiasm."

FROM: WARNER BROS. STUDIOS   BURBANK, CALIF.   H09-1251   CARL COMBS

James Dean, who plays a moody, defiant young man in Warner Bros.' CinemaScope production, "East of Eden," has his own formula for getting into the proper depressed state for each scene. He turns out the lights in his portable dressing room and plays sad music on his record player. Two of his favorites are "Last Spring" and "Heart Wounds" by Grieg.

Elia Kazan is directing and producing "East of Eden" for Warner Bros.

FROM: WARNER BROS. STUDIOS   BURBANK, CALIF.   H09-1251

Hollywood is just getting to know James Dean, who was surrounded with the mysterious air of a Greta Garbo during the making of "East of Eden" at Warner Bros. The "I want to be alone" girl had nothing on Dean, who remained very much to himself.

Director-producer Elia Kazan wouldn't permit newspapermen to interview Dean during production. He didn't want anything to interfere with the young actor's concentration in his screen debut.

When not actively engaged in filming with co-stars – Julie Harris, Raymond Massey and Richard Davalos – Dean was likely to spend the time in his dressing room, listening to classical music. It kept him in the mood for his role of Cal, the moody and troublesome brother in "East of Eden."

In reality Dean sincerely likes people. However, giving the best possible performance meant so much to him that he didn't want any distracting influence. He felt there was something of himself in the character. To reveal honestly the things in the role that were of himself as well as the character was a great challenge.

Co-workers at Warner Bros. came to know and like Dean at the completion of the picture, though he still definitely falls into the category of an off-beat character. He even has attended some Hollywood parties and is seen occasionally at night clubs with beautiful actresses.

At one time he was linked romantically with Pier Angeli. He still prefers to date actresses because he is able to talk shop with them.

FROM: WARNER BROS. STUDIOS   BURBANK, CALIF.   H09-1251   ASHTON

A lot of strange things have happened in Hollywood, but none stranger than the case of James Dean, a squint-eyed young man who has become the season's most important new star and has yet to be seen on the screen.

The word has traveled down the line-that-counts – i.e., from executive producer to fervid fan – that Dean has stardom etched all over his dirty leather jacket.

"Apparently," sniffed one movie-maker, "Warner Bros. has discovered uranium."

The discovery by Warner and Director Elia Kazan of Uranium Dean, however, isn't so unusual as the remarkable circumstance that the fans have also discovered him, pressed him to their bountiful bosom, and made him a star without ever having seen him on the motion picture screen.

It's true that his few television appearances, plus a couple of Broadway roles, have helped to lift the veil of complete professional obscurity from the talented young man. But this wouldn't account for the coast-to-coast recognition he is getting as a full-fledged movie star.

"Warner Bros. Publicity Department churned out stories for the press on every film they made. Even in these earliest press releases, the image of James Dean, the troubled youth/actor begins to take shape. These Hollywood-hardened studio publicists realised Warner Bros. had discovered a unique talent that couldn't be described in old-fashioned show biz press jargon … and the legend begins."

"A great many people, including members of our craft, seem to feel that Jimmy had some sort of secret weapon or magic formula. I do not go along with this. I know that if anyone was ever dedicated to the art of acting, it was Jimmy. He had the greatest power of concentration I have ever encountered. He prepared himself so well in advance for any scene he was playing, that the lines were not simply something he had memorised – they were actually a very real part of him. Before the take of any scene, he would go off by himself for five or ten minutes and think about what he had to do, to the exclusion of everything else. He returned when he felt he was enough in character to shoot the scene."

JIM BACKUS

REBEL · WITHOUT · A · CAUSE

TITLE: "REBEL WITHOUT CAUSE"   DATE: 3-2-55

JIM	JUDY	JIM'S FATHER	JIM'S MOTHER
James Dean	Debby Reynolds	Tony Ross	Ruth Swanson
Tab Hunter	Natalie Wood	Walter Matthau	Mae Clarke
John Kerr	Carol Baker	Bruce Bennett	Peggy Converse
R.J. Wagner	Girls tested or	Harry Townes	Dorothy Green
	discussed:	Rod Cameron	Mary Field
	Susan Whitney	Vaughn Taylor	Ann Doran
	Gloria Castillo	Les Tremayne	Adrienne Marden
	Pat Crowley	Glen Gordon	Katherine Warren
	Kathryn Grant	Raymond Burr	Greta Granstedt
	Cecile Rodgers	Hume Cronyn	Frances Morris
	Nancy Baker	Jeff Morrow	Virginia Christine
	Georgette Michelle	Philip Ober	Phyllis Stanley
	Laurie Stein	Lee Bowman	Mary Baer
	Liza Gaye	Willard Parker	Vivi Janiss
	Melinda Markey	Royal Dano	Benay Venuta
	Sharon Moffatt	Dick Foran	Sylvia Sydney
	Mylee Andreason	Frank Faylen	Natalie Schaefer
	Steffanie Sydney	John Dehner	
	Gigi Perreau		

JUDY'S FATHER	JUDY'S or PLATO'S MOTHER
Brad Dexter	Jeanette Nolan
John Griggs	Joan Banks
Shepard Strudwick	Irene Hervey
Whit Conners	Sally Blaine
Hugh Beaumont	Marsha Hunt
Bruce Bennett	Erin O'Brien-Moore
Everett Sloane	Virginia Huston
Carleton Young	Ann Dvorak
Hayden Rorke	Rochelle Hudson
Warner Anderson	Ruth Hussey
John Archer	Ann Morrison
John Baragrey	Dorothy Bruce
Donald Curtis	Peggy Compton
Bill Hopper	Arlene Whelan
Dick Simmons	Maureen Staple
Leif Erickson	Martha Scott
Doug Kennedy	Evelyn Scott
Hugh Marlowe	Evelyn Keyes
Edward Binns	Irene Collette
Glen Langden	Dorothy Patrick
Richard Denning	Evelyn Ankers
Charles Victor	Henny Backus

175 Rev. 2/53

WARNER BROS.   URES. INC
BURBANK, CALIFORNIA

INTER-OFFICE COMMUNICATION

DATE   March 1, 1955

SUBJECT   "REBEL WITHOUT A CAUS
TESTS - Contd.

-2-

In this light, the love scene in the mansion should be improved.

Actors:

Keeping in mind that whatever known qualities possessed by the actors involved in the test were ignored, in the same way that little attention was paid to makeup or wardrobe, there is only one girl who has shown the capacity to play Judy, and she is Natalie Wood.

At this point, Jeff Silver and Billy Gray are the best candidates for Plato. (Dennis Hopper – only after a test with Jimmy Dean.)

Corey Allen
Nick Adams
Jack Grinnage
Dennis Hopper
Frank Mazzola
Norma Jean Nelson
Tony Mazzola
Ben Gary
Steffi Sidney

Doyle Baker
Butch Cavell
Jerry Olkin
Ken Miller
Bruce Barton
Peter Miller
Nancy Baker
Beverly Long

Gloria Castillo has unmistakable talent and sho
nd for future young character roles. I do
ows for much beyond character at this

STAFF

Producer	David Weisbart	709-710
Director	Nick Ray	771-772
Asst.Dir.	Don Page - 4355 Clybourn, N.H.	SU 23150
2nd Asst.Dir.	Robert Farfan - 1752 N.Whitley Ave., Ho.	HO 98454
Script Super.	Howard Hohler - 131 S. Avon St., Burbank	TH 28955
Cameraman	Ernest Haller - 609 N. Doheny Dr., B.H.	CR 47282
Operator	Bill Shurr - 19526 Ventura Blvd.,Tarzana	DI 32708
Asst.Camera	Stewart Higgs - 11036 Moorpark St., N.H.	SU 21285
Stillman	Floyd McCarty - 9856 Sunland Blvd., Sunland	FL 35352
Art Director	Malcolm Bert - 436 E. Fairview Blvd.,Inglewood	OR 81446
Editor	James Moore - 8862 Wonderland Ave., Ho.	HO 52638
Mixer	Stanley Jones - 4536 Arcola St., N.H.	SU 13754
Prop Man	Herbert Plews - 3119 Valley Heart Blvd.,Bur.VICTORIA	91817
Asst.Prop Man	Robert Turner - 10512 8th Place, Inglewood	PL 51652
Set Dresser	William Wallace - 3100 Clark St., Burbank	TH 62959
Gaffer	Victor Johnson - 350 Mesa Drive, S.M.	EX 56297
Best Boy	Claude Swanner - 10864 Blix, N.H.	SU 11793
Head Grip	Kenneth Taylor - 5809 Lemp, N.H.	SU 24001
Best Boy	George Wilson - 1719 N. Landis, Bur.	TH 64371
Men's Wdbe.	Leon Roberts - 7570½ DeLongpre Ave., Ho.	HO 50011
" "	Henry Field - 424½ N. Ardmore, L.A.	NO 50701
Women's Wdbe.	Marguerite Royce - 704 N. Westmount, W.L.A.	CR 14445
Makeup	Henry Vilardo - 6655 Allott Ave., V.N.	ST 68105
Hairdresser	Tillie Starriett - 5446 Woodman Ave., V.N.	ST 54494

CAST

Jim	James Dean - 1541 Sunset Plaza Dr., Ho.	HO 75191
Jim's Grandmother		
Jim's Father	Jim Backus - 1521 Linda Crest, B.H.	CR 14126
Jim's Mother	Marsha Hunt - 13151 Magnolia Blvd., V.N.	ST 40463
Judy	Natalie Wood - 15036 Valley Vista Blvd., S.O.	ST 99708
Judy's Father	Bill Hopper - 7050 Lasaine, V.N.	DI 21953
Judy's Mother		
Beau		
Plato	Sal Mineo - 4918 Rhodes Ave., N.H.	SU 22375
Buzz	Corey Allen - 10632½ Wilshire Blvd., W.L.A.	GR 83452
Helen	Beverly Long - 9040 Dix St., Ho.	CR 55564
Marsha		
Ginger		
Crunch	Frank Mazzola - 1520 N. Ogden Drive, Ho.	HO 75657
Moose	Jack Simmons -	HO 33952

(CONTINUED)

Mr. J. L. Warner   March 31, 1955
Warner Bros. Pictures, Inc.
Burbank, California

Dear Mr. Warner:

    We have read the final script dated March 25, for
your picture REBEL WITHOUT A CAUSE, and are happy to
note the changes and improvements made therein of the
first version. As discussed with Mr. MaDermid over the
telephone there remain certain minor items which we
believe need further correction. We list these below.

    Page 6: The dialogue beginning "Did you stop to
talk to anyone, Judy" still suggests that this sixteen-
year old girl has been brought in for soliciting. This
objectionable flavor is unacceptable.

    Page 28: In this scene of the high-school girls
"sneaking a smoke" there should be no suggestion that
they are smoking marijuana.

    Page 43: If this knife-duel is to be approved it
will have to be treated without too much emphasis, and
not shown in too much detail. Also, on this page, the
action of Buzz kicking Plato when he is down will have
to be omitted.

    Page 50: In order to avoid any questionable flavor
to this scene, we urge that Judy do not actually kiss
her father on the lips, but only move towards him with
this in mind, which will bring about his reaction. This
will omit the actual kiss.

    Page 65: We again urge the advisability of not
suggesting that these kids in their auto racing are
endangering innocent passengers on the highway below.

    Page 77: We again urge the importance of not
suggesting that these highschool kids consider going
in for murder. We feel that this objectionable flavor
has not been entirely removed.

Page 85: The dialogue beginning "Have you ever gone with anyone who" and ending "Isn't that awful" is unacceptable as a frank admission to sexual immorality on the part of these high-school pupils.

Page 91: We again suggest avoiding the flavor that these high-school boys are out for murder. Possibly changing Jim's line "We know" would avoid this.

Page 99: It will be absolutely essential that this scene be handled very carefully so that there will be no suggestion of a sex affair between Jim and Judy. Its acceptability will depend entirely on how it will come through in the finished picture. We believe it would help if the scene end in a note of tenderness, omitting the second kiss by Jim.

Page 101: We suggest merely indicating that these high-school boys have tire chains, not showing them flaunting them.

Page 102: We suggest the possibility of not having Plato actually fire his gun on Jim. Jim might wrestle with him and the gun go off.

Page 103: It will be very important when Judy appears that there be nothing about her appearance or actions that suggests that there has been a previous sex affair between her and Jim. The same, of course, applies to Jim's appearance on the previous page.

You understand, of course, that our final judgment will be based on the finished picture.

Cordially yours,

Geoffrey M. Shurlock

Lithograph Billing _ _ "REBEL WITHOUT A CAUSE" _ _ _ _ August 12, 1955

(NOTE: This credit must be 50%)	WARNER BROS.	50%
	Pictures Presents	5%
No adv. Obligation.	JAMES DEAN	100%
	"REBEL WITHOUT A CAUSE"	100%
	Also Starring	
CONTRACT: Must be 1st fea. on scr. In adv., except 4-col. inches or less.	NATALIE WOOD	40%
	with	
	SAL MINEO	25%
	JIM BACKUS	15%
	ANN DORAN	15%
No adv. obligation.	COREY ALLEN	15%
	WILLIAM HOPPER	15%

NOTE: Size of fea. players at your discretion.

	in CinemaScope	50%
	and WarnerColor	50%
Writing credit need not appear in group, teaser or ads less than 8 col. inches. See Basic Agrmt. for other exceptions.	Screen Play by Stewart Stern	15%
Producer credit need not appear in group, teaser or ads less than 8 col. inches. See Basic Agrmt. for other exceptions.	Produced by David Weisbart	15%
Director credit need not appear in group, teaser or ads less than 4 column inches. See Basic Agrmt. for other exceptions.	Directed by Nicholas Ray	15%
R E V I S E D F I N A L B I L L I N G	A Warner Bros. Picture	5%

* * *

(AS O.K.'D BY J.L.WARNER)

8-12-55

March 30, 1955 – *Rebel Without a Cause*

begins production. James Dean as Jim Stark –

the definitive troubled youth. "J.D. … James Dean!

Juvenile Delinquent! … Just Dynamite!"

WARNER BROS. NEWSPAPER AD

REBEL WITHOUT A CAUSE – 1955

"Well, then, there, now, were you having a ball, Dad?" Jim Stark to his father (Jim Backus), as

mother, (Ann Doran), looks up to her fallen son in rehearsal.

Peering into the caged office that holds Plato (Sal Mineo), Jim Stark already

shows his concern for this frightened rabbit/child.

Director Nicholas Ray observes the first confrontation scene between Jim Stark, his parents, Ray, and juvenile police officer (Edward Platt).

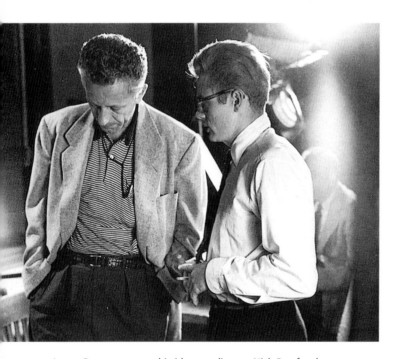

James Dean expresses his ideas to director Nick Ray for the

highly emotional scene coming up.

Even in rehearsal, James Dean's pent-

up energies simmer and seethe ...

… until they finally explode before the camera. Emotions taking over, he attacks the desk, nearly demolishing his hands. Here Edward Platt goads Jim into action as Dean's fight coach, Mushy Callahan, watches in stunned silence.

From: Warner Bros. Studio
Burbank, Calif...HO 9-1251

Halperin

James Dean suffered a badly bruised right hand today (22) while doing a scene in Warner Bros.' "Rebel Without A Cause."

Dean slammed his right fist into the side of a desk a little harder then the script called for.

He was taken to Riverside Drive Emergency Hospital where x-rays revealed no broken bones.

Dean will have to keep his hand wrapped in an elastic bandage for at least a week, but the injured hand will not prevent him from working.

-o-

H. Carroll
/3

Between takes. "Rebel without a comb."

Jim Stark finishes breakfast before his first day at a new school in a new town.

"Even if Jimmy doesn't have a line to speak, I feel he's talking to me. I can tell by the way he looks, the movement of his hands, the slight motion of his facial muscles."
NATALIE WOOD
WARNER BROS.
PUBLICITY RELEASE
HALPERIN: 5/23/55

James Dean rehearses his arrival at "Dawson High School".
In the first photograph, Dean is being berated for stepping on
the school seal. In the second, Dean looks to Nick Ray for
direction. In the third, producer David Weisbart
helps Jimmy with his script.

On the balcony of the planetarium, James Dean and Sal Mineo look down into

the parking lot where the gang waits for them.

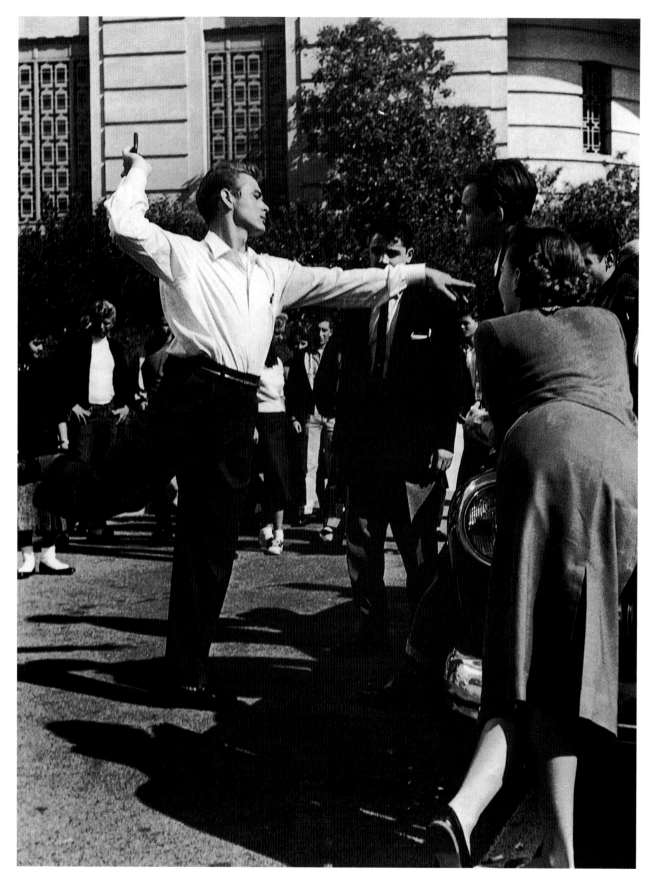

During rehearsal, James Dean surprises his co-stars Sal, Corey and Natalie, by assuming a danseur's pose,

complete with a tire-iron in his hand.

"I've never met anyone with the
ability of Dean. He cannot be
compared with any actor, present
or past. I'm sure he'll bring
performances to the screen the
likes of which haven't yet been
thought of."
NICK RAY WARNER BROS.
PUBLICITY RELEASE
HALPERIN; 5/23/55

"You know, I'll bet you're a
real yo-yo." Judy (Natalie
Wood) to Jim (James Dean).
Rebel Without a Cause

ACCIDENT RECORD

R BROS. PICTURES, INC.   REPORT OF "REFERRED" CASES--FOR APRIL 1955   DEPT. TALENT
(WEST COAST STUDIOS)

NAME	EXTENT OF INJURY	CAUSE OF ACCIDENT	STUDIO OR LOCATION	FOREMAN	DOCTOR
			Studio	Ray	Dr. Hiatt
n, J.	Cont. rt. hand	Struck desk in scene	San Francisco	Tuttle	Dr. Hiatt
si, L.	Cont. top head	Struck in fight scene	Studio	Tuttle	St. Josephs
xley, P.	Lac. rt. palm	Struck in fight scene			

COPIES TO

____ DEPARTMENT HEAD
____ INSURANCE DEPARTMENT
____ INSURANCE COMPANY
____ INSURANCE BROKER
____ FILE
BM 11-53 WL

The hands of Nick Ray direct Jimmy while Corey Allen holds his position for the knife-fight scene.

In rehearsal for the knife-fight ballet.

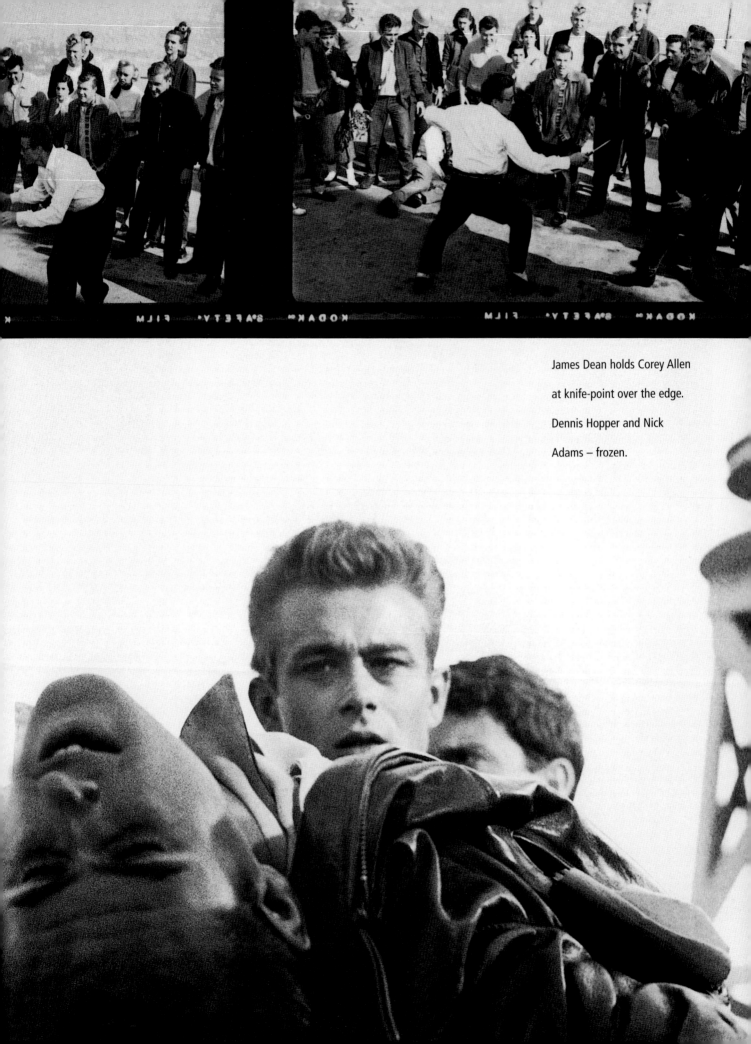

James Dean holds Corey Allen

at knife-point over the edge.

Dennis Hopper and Nick

Adams – frozen.

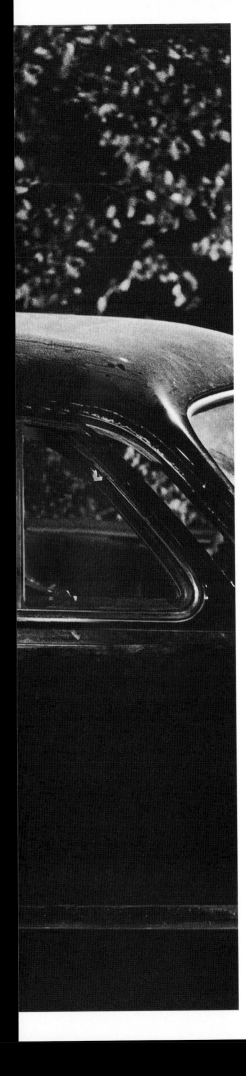

Plato (Sal Mineo) greets Jim
(James Dean) upon his arrival at
the site of the "Chickie Run".

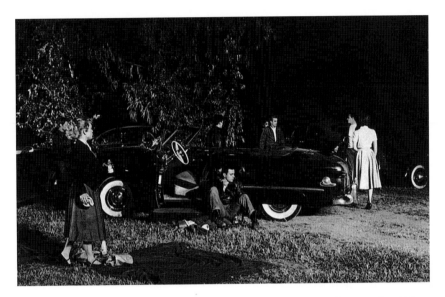

The fifties … fast cars, fast kids,
fast times. Jim and Buzz meet for
a duel to the death.

The start of the "Chickie Run".
Jim asks Judy for the same luck
she just gave Buzz.

"He knows what he's doing all the time. He pounces on lines and devours them as if they were the substance of life."

ANN DORAN WARNER BROS. PUBLICITY RELEASE HALPERIN: 5/23/55

In this photograph, following the "Chickie Run", James Dean and Frank Mazzola trade punches before Dean's entrance into the police station. In the film, they trade only words.

Rehearsing …

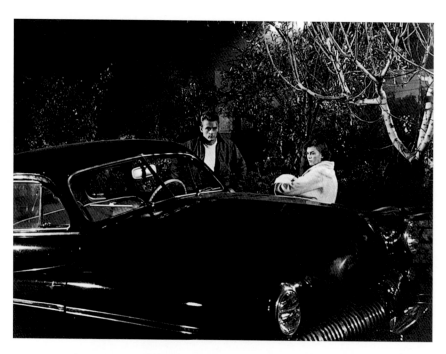

James Dean and Natalie Wood, a couple of misunderstood kids,

solving their problems on their own.

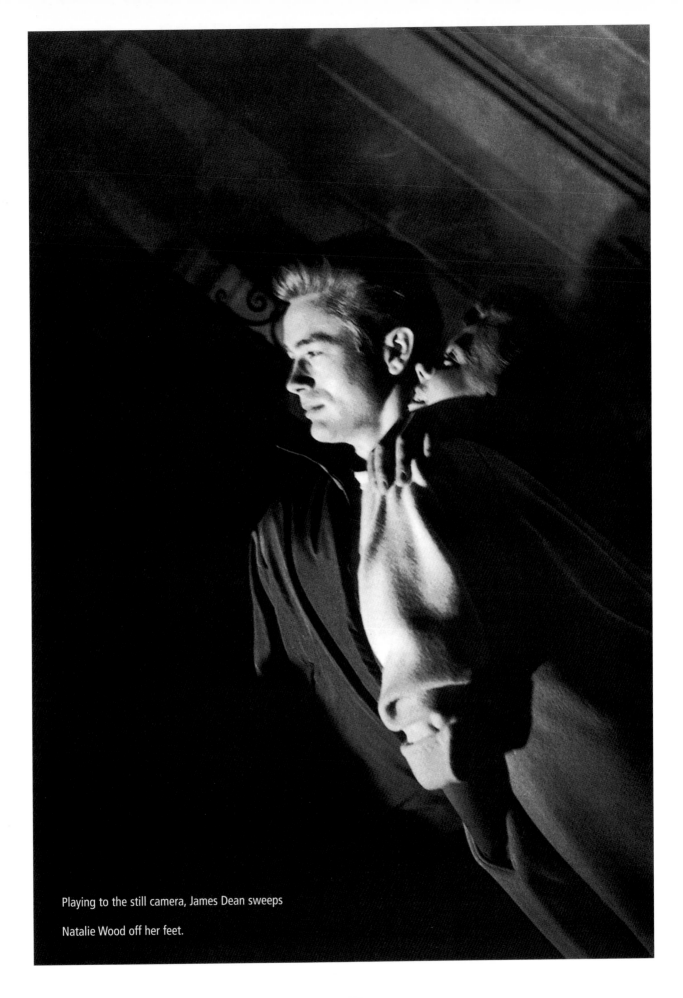

Playing to the still camera, James Dean sweeps
Natalie Wood off her feet.

Inside the mansion, Jim Stark asks Plato, the outsider, for the "password".

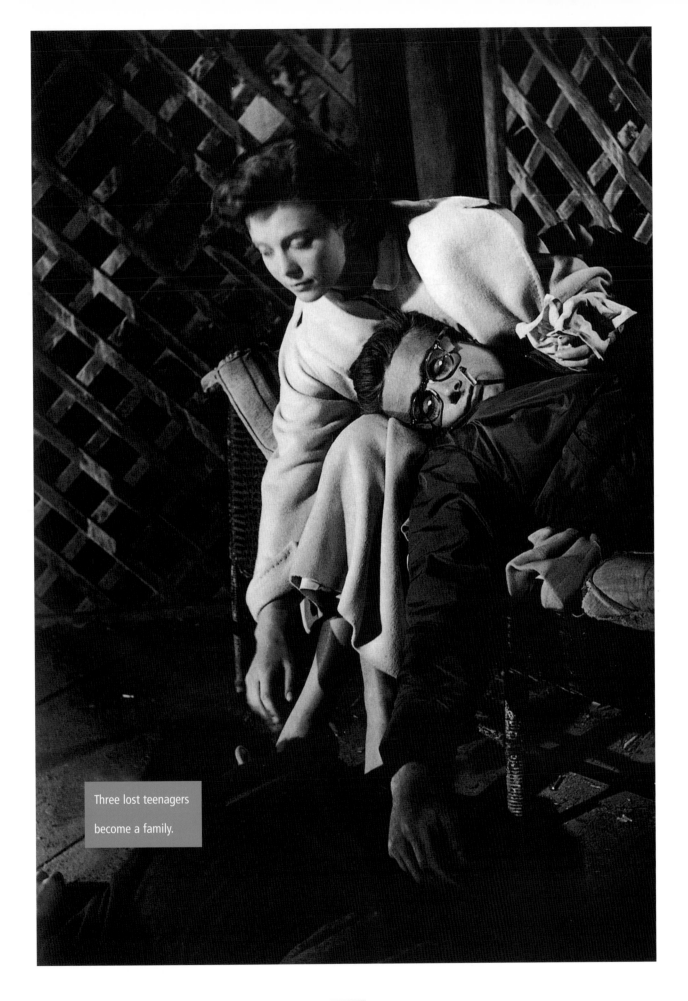

Three lost teenagers
become a family.

Natalie laughs …   … Jimmy collapses …

… and Jim and Judy fall in love.

Chasing Plato – Jim and Judy on the run from the police.

James Dean …

in the night.

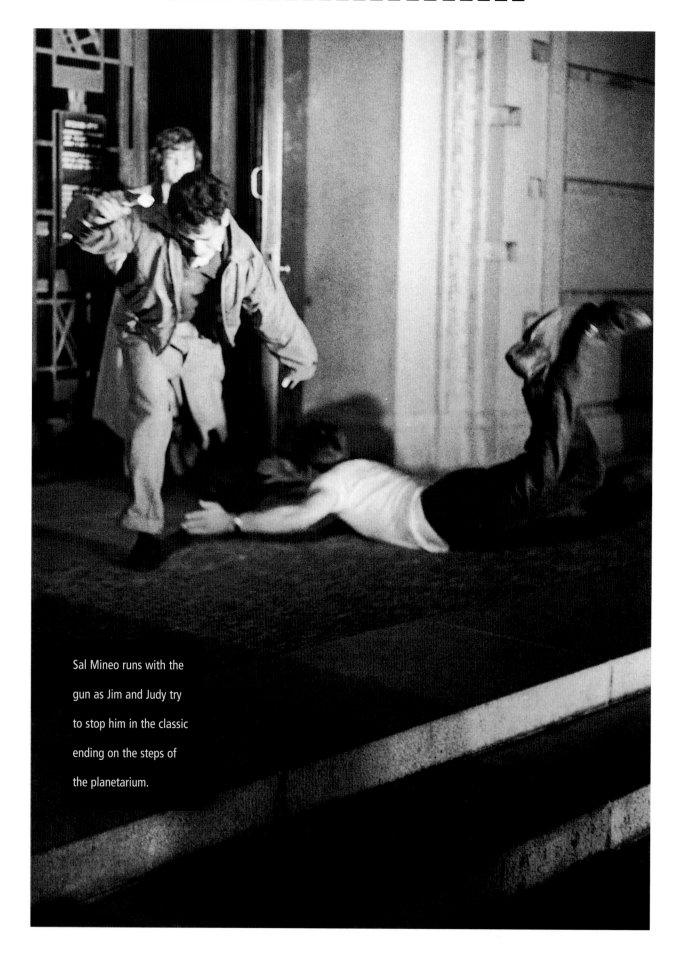

Sal Mineo runs with the
gun as Jim and Judy try
to stop him in the classic
ending on the steps of
the planetarium.

"I've got the bullets!"

The original ending … Dean "directs" Sal Mineo and Natalie Wood in the

daylight run to the roof of the planetarium.

The original ending …

"I've got …

"… the bullets!"

Again – "I've got …

… the bullets!"

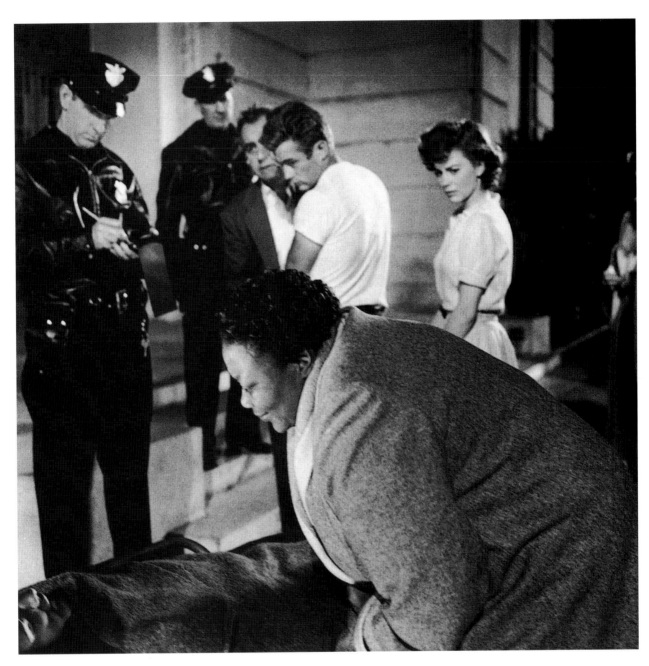

One family dies and another family is reborn. James Dean, Jim Backus and

Natalie Wood watch Louise Beavers tend the fallen Sal Mineo.

FORM 11

WARNER BROS. PICTURES, INC.
BURBANK, CALIFORNIA

INTER-OFFICE COMMUNICATION

TO MR. J. L. Warner

FROM MR. Nicholas Ray

DATE June 7, 1955

SUBJECT "REBEL WITHOUT A CAUSE"

Dear Jack:

My name is Nick Ray and I just finished making a picture for you called REBEL WITHOUT A CAUSE. I thought maybe you'd forgotten my name because the last time we met any closer than bowing distance was in your office late at night and you wished you'd never met me and I thought you should have felt just the opposite. At that time you threatened with another such meeting if anything else went wrong, and while I _know_ you must have been pissed off at me at least once – and strongly enough to have called another meeting – there hasn't been another such meeting. So either you've forgotten my name or else you have the kind of understanding a director dreams about.

If that's the case, I could use some more (understanding – that is). Here's the problem. We have a lot of footage. (I'm telling you – all right.) Some of it I haven't even seen due to my hours of work, and lack of contact with the cutter. But I know every important frame of it as if it had been printed on my skin, including the out-takes and the unprinted prints. I've seen a couple sequences slapped together for an expediency of one sort or another (with takes in wrong places and the wrong parts of takes in other places, etc., etc.) and yet, because I do know what we have, I come out of the projection room feeling better than the law allows.

Last week, while the cutter was assembling, Dave and I were occupied with post-syncing in order to get Dean off to Texas. The picture was not available and it still isn't completely together.

Yesterday, Dave and I had our first chance to <u>start</u> on our rough
out. I'd like us to have enough time to put together a version
which I feel will represent the best of the material on hand from
which we can all go ahead together into our final version. We would
be eliminating those things which you shouldn't have to waste your
time with and which we all would find distracting to the overall
picture.

I'm not talking about any drawn-out procedure. I can't. Every
added day from here on costs me money. For I'm due on another
picture immediately and do not feel I can officially report to them.
But I think we have a wonderful show, and I would like your first
viewing of it to contain as much of its true value as we can get in
even a limited but not unreasonable amount of time.

July 1st, 1955

Dear Steve:

        Be sure to instruct Weisbart
and Rosenman and all concerned with music
on REBEL WITH A CAUSE. As I said last
night it is one of the most important
factors in the picture especially the last
third. Do not let them go "arty" on us.

        I sent Benny the following wire:

    "SAW FIRST ROUGH CUT OF REBEL WITH A
    CAUSE LAST NIGHT. THE PICTURE ITSELF
    IS EXCELLENT. DEAN IS BEYOND
    COMPREHENSION."

        That's how I feel although there
are places to make it move about which all
of us are aware.

        See if the boys can get this ready
for a preview before I leave. It is very
imperative that they do as I will explain when
I see you.

                        JACK

WARNER BROS.
PICTURES
DISTRIBUTING CORPORATION
1307 S. WABASH AVE.   CHICAGO 5, ILL.
PHONE HARRISON 7-6052

OCTOBER 26,1955

Mr A S Howson
New York

Dear Mr Howson

Confirming our telephone conversation of today, the following
cuts are to be made in REBEL WITHOUT A CAUSE:

1 - KNIFE FIGHT - CUT ACTUAL FIGHTING TO A MINIMUM

2 - CUT SCENE SHOWING JIM WITH KNIFE AT BUZZ' THROAT

3 - CUT SCENE CHOKING OF FATHER (ACTUAL CHOKING)

Would appreciate hearing from you as soon as possible.

Thanks and kind regards -

Yours very truly,

George Lefko.

GL MC.

"This Sept. 2 1955 telegram from Steve Trilling firmly establishes James Dean's stardom."

TRILLING TO MAJOR WARNER, KALMENSON, SCHNEIDER AND COHEN

HAD EXCITING PREVIEW REBEL WITHOUT CAUSE HUNTINGTON PARK LAST NIGHT. AUDIENCE REACTION ON SIGHT OF HIS NAME AND APPEARANCE PROVED CONCLUSIVELY JAMES DEAN STRONG IMPORTANT STAR UP THERE WITH MARLON BRANDO. STORY PERFORMANCES ENTIRE PICTURE RECEIVED EXCELLENTLY. BEN WALLERSTEIN WHO WAS THERE IN ADDITION TO BEING ENTHUSIASTIC OVER PICTURE PREDICTED WOULD BE TREMENDOUS BOXOFFICE WILL RUSH THROUGH QUICKLY AS POSSIBLE SO YOU CAN HAVE PRINT SOON NEWYORK

ER BROS.
URES. INC.
COAST STUDIOS
BANK. CALIFORNIA

September 7, 1955

Mr. Wolfe Cohen
Warner Bros. Pictures, Inc.
321 West 44th Street
New York, New York

Dear Wolfe:

Thanks your letter September 2nd...and I was very happy to hear your reaction to the trailer for "REBEL WITHOUT A CAUSE". Am conveying your thoughts to the Trailer Department...particularly that this is the "type" trailer that you like for foreign use.

Re your other letter of September 2nd with attached copy letter from the Chief Censor, Commonwealth of Australia. I fully appreciate your concern; however would like you to know that we previewed "REBEL WITHOUT A CAUSE" at Huntington Park last Thursday and there was none of the "shock" reaction we would normally get at a showing of a gangster or "BLACKBOARD JUNGLE" type picture. Our picture, "REBEL", has elements showing the problems besetting American youth and the leaning toward delin- quency induced by lack of understanding between parent and child, but it completely lacks any of the homicidal tendencies indicated in other films...and I think this might prove the exception to the rule.

I am not certain if you saw the rough cut sent to New York three or four weeks ago, but the final American version should be ready within the next few weeks -- I would appreciate your viewing the print and then judge if you want to make any censor cuts for your foreign exhibition prior to shipping abroad. I repeat...it is difficult to make comparisons as it hasn't the extreme violence of "BLACKBOARD JUNGLE" nor does it show the extreme unsavory special groups of characters. However, we share your concern maintaining our foreign market and I would like your comments after you see the film. It is possible we can eliminate some of the elements that might bother you or might create an adverse situation--particularly the knife fight.

All best...

As ever,

Steve T....

WARNER
WARDOUR STREET,
LONDON, W.I.

November 28th 1955.

REF :
ASA/WC/55-84

Mr. Wolfe Cohen,
New York.

Dear Wolfe,

I have received your letter of November 22nd and will attempt to bring you up to date on the REBEL WITHOUT A CAUSE censorship situation.

After very cleverly eliminating the entire knife fight, reducing shots of the girl's excitement before the car race, and making several minor cuts here and there, we got an **X** certificate for the film.

I objected to this, resubmitted it and asked for an A grading. On Friday I received the Censor's specifications for an A certificate (which are attached) and which I feel are excessive.

In discussing the matter with Goodlatte and Stack, I have come to the conclusion that we should proceed with our **X** and leave the picture alone.   This will cost us twenty or thirty thousand pounds, but to have a picture which makes no sense would cost us more, and I still think we can go over £100,000.

I have just arranged for a booking early in the New Year for the Pavilion -- the West End home of **X** certificates -- and will probably get a March date on the A.B.C. circuit.

I'm sorry that I allowed Nick Ray to get into this situation, but I did so on the off chance that he could impress Watkins, the Censor, by his sincerity about the moral tone of the film.   He cut absolutely no ice with him, however, and in last week's Variety I read some stuff about the censorship problems on the film which could only have come from Ray. I make a very strong point of keeping completely mum with the press on our problems with the Censor.   By exposing them we might win a couple of decisions, but in the long run he'd make us sorry we talked, so all our differences are kept strictly between us.

December   5th,   1955

Mr. Wolfe Cohen
Warner Bros. Pictures, Inc.
321 West 44th Street
New York, New York

Dear Wolfe:

Thanks for your letter of December 2nd with the letter from Abeles and the letter he received from the English censor on REBEL WITHOUT A CAUSE.

Abeles did the right thing.   To mutilate the film in order to satisfy the Censor for an "A" certificate, would destroy the entire picture.   If there are any repercussions on this, will appreciate hearing from you.   It's too bad the English censors do not realize that by showing the truth on the screen, they can correct the evils of both parents and children.   They should let the pictures mirror life.   I am positive that's how it works in our country.   I know the results obtained when gangsters were shown in their true light were very enlightening.   However, I am sure our pictures will not be the cause of changing English censorship.

Re: Nick Ray, I never have permitted Producers, Directors or Writers to interfere.   Unfortunately, Ray happened to be in London and I was under the impression he could be of some help.   We will return to our policy of letting Producers, Directors and Writers make the films and we will sell them.

as far as I am conc

"Meanwhile, foreign censors were proving more difficult to please than their American counterparts. In these exchanges, Steve Trilling, Arthur Abeles and Jack L. Warner discuss the problems in Australia and England."

FROM: WARNER BROS. STUDIOS   BURBANK, CALIF.   H09-1251   HALPERIN

(One minute interview with James Dean at a preview of Warner Bros.' "Rebel Without a Cause.")

Since I'm only 24 years old, guess I have as good an insight into this rising generation as any other young man my age. And I've discovered that most young men do not stand like ramrods or talk like Demosthenes. Therefore, when I do play a youth, such as in Warner Bros.' "Rebel Without a Cause," I try to imitate life. The picture deals with the problems of modern youth. It is the romanticised conception of the juvenile that causes much of our trouble with misguided youth nowadays. I think one thing this picture shows that's new is the psychological disproportion of the kids' demands on the parents. Parents are often at fault, but the kids have some work to do, too. But you can't show some far-off idyllic conception of behavior if you want the kids to come and see the picture. You've got to show what it's really like, and try and reach them on their own grounds. You know, a lot of times an older boy, one of the fellows the young ones idolize, can go back to the high school kids and tell them, "Look what happened to me! Why be a punk and get in trouble with the law? Why do these senseless things just for a thrill?" I hope "Rebel Without a Cause" will do something like that. I hope it will remind them that other people have feelings. Perhaps they will say "What do we need all that for?" If a picture is psychologically motivated, if there is truth in the relationship in it, then I think that picture will do good. I firmly believe that "Rebel Without a Cause" is such a picture.

FROM: WARNER BROS. STUDIOS   BURBANK, CALIF.   H09-1251

James Dean has so many off-the-screen activities he says he may have to drop some in order to concenrate on acting.

"After all, acting is my first love," he said at Warner Bros. where he's starring in "Rebel Without a Cause", a youth drama in CinemaScope and WarnerColor.

Dean, an expert bongo player before he came to Hollywood to star in "East of Eden", has added sport car racing, bull fighting, skin diving and motion picture photography to his interests.

"With so many outside pursuits, I'm afraid my acting will suffer," he said. "Only problem is I don't know which to abandon – at least temporarily."

Dean is not only one of the hottest acting talents in Hollywood today, but he's also called one of the best sport car race drivers to compete in Southern California circles in years.

He stunned veteran sport car fans when he tooled his Porsche roadster to victories in the Palm Springs and Bakersfield National Road Races – the only events he's entered so far. He has five trophies for his winning efforts.

Not content with these ventures Dean, who admits he wants to be a film director some day, has purchased more than $2000 worth of motion picture camera equipment with which he expects to produce two-reel short subjects in the near future.

"My contract with Warner Bros. calls for nine pictures in six years. That means I'll have to direct all my energies toward acting," Dean said.

"I think I'll stick with sport car racing and motion picture photography. I already have a sport car and there's no use giving it up. And since I want to be a film director, my motion picture equipment will aid me in that endeavour."

However, Dean is quick to add that actors, like other professional people, need outside hobbies.

"Anyone who dedicates himself to one job soon finds himself in a rut," he said. "I find it refreshing to engage in my avocations. Anyway, if I fail as an actor, I'll have something to fall back on," he added.

"James Dean was a dedicated, perfectionist actor. I watched him develop bits of business until they seemed a part of his nature. He asked cowboys to teach him intricate tricks with a rope. He worked himself bleary-eyed with that rope, but if you watch him as Jett Rink doing tricks with that rope in *Giant*, you will see a Texas boy who has been working with a rope all his cotton-pickin' life! I watched him learn how to let his hat fall from his head, watched it do a complete somersault and land, top side up, on the ground in front of him … just the way he wanted it! Every time he did it.

While he was playing Jett Rink, he was inseparable from Jett Rink; he did NOT become Jett Rink, but Jett Rink was his constant companion!"

MERCEDES McCAMBRIDGE

(McCambridge, Mercedes The Quality of Mercy: An Autobiography *Times Books New York 1981)*

GIANT

JORDAN BENEDICT

John Wayne
Gregory Peck
Errol Flynn
Burt Lancaster
Robert Taylor
Jeff Chandler
Kirk Douglas
Cornel Wilde
Tyrone Power
Robert Mitchum
Guy Madison
Victor Mature
Glen Ford
Charlton Heston
Sterling Hayden
Joel McCrea
Joe Cotten
Henry Fonda
Bill Holden
James Stewart
Alan Ladd

LESLIE

Jane Wyman
Jenifer Jones
Grace Kelly
Olivia DeHaviland
Ava Gardner
Susan Hayward
Jean Simmons
Eleanor Parker
Maureen O'Hara
Vivian Leigh
Elizabeth Taylor
Virginia Mayo
Rita Hayworth
Deborah Kerr
Ann Blyth
Jane Greer
Donna Reid
Audrey Hepburn
Kathryn Hepburn
Ann Baxter
June Allyson
Gene Tierney
Shelley Winters
Joan Dru
Gloria Grahame

JETT RINK

Marlon Brando
James Whitmore
Robert Mitchum
Charlton Heston
Cornel Wilde
Tony Quinn
Steve Cochrane
Richard Widmark
Richard Basehart
George Nader
Monty Clift
Van Heflin
Steve McNally
Robert Preston
Jerome Thor
John Hodiak
Robert Ryan
Jack Palance
John Ireland
Richard Conti
Howard Duff

LUZ SR.

Tallulah Bankhead
Judith Anderson
Mildred Dunneck
Katherine Empry
Ann Harding
Jessica Tandy
Frieda Inescourt
Sara Hayden
Angela Lansbury
Doris Packer
Katherine Warren
Agnes Moorhead
Nana Bryant
Aline McMahon
Edith Meiser
Blanche Yurka
Betty Field
Grace Hartman
Una Merkel
Millie Natwick
Dorothy Stickney
Marglo Gilmord
Margaret Hayes
Jessie Royce Landis

JORDAN JR.

James Best
Paul Burke
Don Keefer
Tyler McDuff
Chris Drake
Gil Donaldson
Jack Kelley
Keith Larsen
Leonard Nimoy
Richard Long
John Bromfield
Bill Campbell
Jack Lemmon
Kevin McCarthy
James Mitchell
Paul Richards
John Barrymore Jr.
Ric Jason
John Kerr
Michael Wager
Biff Elliot
Dewey Martin
Tom Drake
Douglas Dick
Gar Moore
Ron Ronell
Darryl Hickman

JUANA

Donna Martell
Mara Corday
Yvette Dugay
Laurette Luez
Rita Moreno
Betta St. John
Barbara James Jake
Anna Marie Albergetti
Pier Angeli
Abbey Lane
Mona Freeman
Joan Taylor
Anna Navarro
Pilar Del Ray
Hillary Hall

LUZ JR.

Martha Hyer
Dawn Adams
Nancy Olsen
Piper Laurie
Vanessa Brown
Mary Sinclair
Jane Greer
Gloria Grahame
Pat Medina
Barbara Britton
Sheila Connely
Gloria De Haven
Jeff Donnell
Peggy Ann Garner
Lee Grant
Julie Harris
Mary Ellen Kay
Barbara Ruick
Eleanor Todd
Joan Dru
Joan Taylor
Ruth Hampton
Connie Smith

VASHTI SAYTH

Check New York
for Names

MOTION PICTURE ASSOCIATION
OF AMERICA, INC.
8480 BEVERLY BOULEVARD
HOLLYWOOD 48, CALIFORNIA
WEbster 3-7101

ERIC JOHNSTON
PRESIDENT

JOSEPH I. BREEN
VICE PRESIDENT AND
DIRECTOR
PRODUCTION CODE ADMINISTRATION

December 13, 1954

Mr. J. L. Warner
Warner Bros. Pictures, Inc.
4000 W. Olive Avenue
Burbank, California

Dear Mr. Warner:

We have read the estimating script for your proposed production, GIANT, and are happy to report that, with the following exceptions, this material seems to meet the requirements of the Production Code.

Page 19: As presently written, Scene 40 seems excessively sex suggestive. This excess of sex suggestiveness stems from the fact that the scene is played in a bedroom, that our principals are attired in night clothes, that it is their wedding night, and that the entire sequence is played in semi-darkness. We suggest that, if the principals were in a sitting position rather than prone on a bed, and if the room were lighted, much of the excessive sex suggestiveness might be eliminated.

Page 61: The expression "Good Lord" is unacceptable.

Page 64: Dr. Walker's expression "I wish to God" is irreverent, and therefore unacceptable.

Page 111: The word "damn" in Uncle Bawley's dialogue is unacceptable.

Page 126: Jett's use of the word "damn" is unacceptable.

Page 145: Bick's use of the word "damn" is unacceptable.

Page 146: The expression "Madre de Dios" is unacceptable.

Page 156: We assume that you will obtain adequate technical advice regarding the portrayal of the marriage ceremony.

Page 170: Bick's expression "Good Lord" is unacceptable.

Page 183: Watts' expression "Lord" is unacceptable.

Page 194: Jordy's expression "Good Lord" and Bick's expression "Lord" are unacceptable.

Page 199: The expression "Madre Dios" is unacceptable.

Page 202: Jett's use of the word "damn" is unacceptable.

Page 211: The fight sequence, as well as other scenes of physical conflict, must be handled with great care in order that there be no excessive brutality or gruesomeness. Of late, our industry has received severe criticism from many quarters for what has been termed our "sadistic love of brutality for its own sake." We strongly urge you to exercise great restraint in this matter in order that we may belie the charge made against our industry of being exploiters of sadism.

Page 214: Bick's expression "Good Lord" is unacceptable.

You understand, of course, that our final judgment will be based on the finished picture.

Cordially yours,

Geoffrey M. Shurlock

P. S. We have also read one changed page (218) dated 12/5/54, for this production, and it seems to be acceptable.

COPY

O MR. HENRY GINSBERG   DATE DECEMBER 14, 1954
GIANT PRODUCTIONS
ROM MR. CARL MILLIKEN, JR.   SUBJECT "GIANT"

CENSORSHIP MEMO

I should explain that the Research Department on this lot is charged with a secondary responsibility; namely, assisting the Legal Department in the examination of scripts with a view to anticipating, if possible, any lawsuits that might arise from our defaming anybody or violating their individual right of privacy. Since Warner Bros. Pictures, Inc. will be a co-defendant in any action brought against an independent producer releasing through Warner Bros., it is our custom to examine the scripts for independent productions in the same way that we would our own.

Edna Ferber's GIANT is a specially worrisome property because it has been accepted, to a large extent, in the public mind as a true document not only of life in Texas but also specifically of the lives of the Kleberg family, which owns and operates the King Ranch, and of Glenn McCarthy, the much publicized Texas oil millionaire. In this connection perhaps we need only to quote from the review of the novel which appeared in the Saturday Review:

> "Despite the disclaimer in the front of
> the book, the characters in "Giant" will
> strike many Texans as bearing a remark-
> able resemblance to actual persons.
> Some will think that this is actually the
> story of the King Ranch and Bob Kleberg,
> and of the Shamrock Hotel and Glenn
> McCarthy, but on closer examination they
> will find they are wrong. Very carefully
> but casually, Miss Ferber brings Bob and
> Glenn and the Shamrock into her narrative,
> thus proving beyond a peradventure of a
> doubt that Glenn McCarthy is Glenn McCarthy
> himself, not Jett Rink, Bick Benedict is
> not Bob Kleberg after all, and the little
> old King Ranch of only a million or so
> acres is definitely not the giant Reata spread
> of which Miss Ferber speaks. It is about as
> difficult to identify the characters and
> places in "Giant" as it would be to recognize
> the Washington Monument if it were painted
> purple."

FORM 11

WARNER BROS. PICTURES. INC.
BURBANK, CALIFORNIA

COPY

INTER-OFFICE COMMUNICATION

To Mr. _____ HENRY GINSBERG _____ Date _____ DECEMBER 14, 1954 _____
             GIANT PRODUCTIONS
From Mr. _____ CARL MILLIKEN, JR. _____ Subject _____ "GIANT" _____

CENSORSHIP MEMO (Cont. Page 4)

Bick says (Scene 105, Page 49), "My old man brought in Herefords from England and bred 'em with the best we had." Although we have already noted the difference concerning Brahman versus "Oriental" stock, it should be remembered that Robert Kleberg's father was the individual in the King dynasty who began the improvement of the range stock. It was he who brought in Herefords; it was the present Kleberg who brought in the Brahman strain.

Benedict (Scene 55) also mentions that his father built the tremendous ranch home. It was Robert Kleberg I, the father of the present Kleberg, who built the Santa Gertrudis Main House, which is an almost exact replica of the house described in Edna Ferber's novel.

Even the size of the two ranches is almost identical. In the script (Scene 17, Page 8) it is mentioned as being "...around a million acres..." The King Ranch in 1933, according to Fortune Magazine, contained 1,250,000 acres. In a like way, the Benedict ranch is described (Scene 347, Page 150) as the "biggest ranching project in the history of the country." Fortune Magazine is again the authority for the fact that the King Ranch is the world's biggest ranch.

(C) JETT RINK is another controversial character for whom a real-life prototype exists; namely, Glenn McCarthy. Both Jett Rink and Glenn McCarthy are poor Texas boys who made a killing through wildcat oil operations. In the script Bick Benedict is portrayed as selling his ranch oil to a company controlled by Jett Rink. In actual fact, both the King Ranch and Glenn McCarthy (at the time he was first wildcatting in oil) sold their oil to the Humble Oil Company, an independent company which is now a subsidiary of Standard of New Jersey. The most telling resemblance between Jett Rink and Glenn McCarthy, of course, is the ownership of a tremendous new hotel. In Jett Rink's case it is the Conquistador, described in the script (Scene 382, Page 162) as "...a twenty-story hotel...a memorable landmark in the history of our great state..." In actuality the Shamrock Hotel built by Glenn McCarthy was eighteen stories, but even bigger.

FORM 11

WARNER BROS. PICTURES. INC.
BURBANK, CALIFORNIA

COPY

INTER-OFFICE COMMUNICATION

TO MR. HENRY GINSBERG   DATE DECEMBER 14, 1954
GIANT PRODUCTIONS
FROM MR. CARL MILLIKEN, JR.   SUBJECT "GIANT"

CENSORSHIP MEMO (Cont. Page 5)

In addition to ownership of such a hotel, there is even
greater danger in the tremendous party which is thrown
for invited guests. It will be remembered by the public
that McCarthy imported planeloads of Hollywood celebrities
and other dignitaries. Jett Rink is shown as doing like-
wise. Hollywood personalities are mentioned as being in
attendance, and (Scene 382, Page 162) Pinky says, "Yeh,
they say you have to have 10 million just to get on the
guest list," whereupon Whiteside replies, "Why, there's
going to be cabinet members from Washington and movie
stars singing..." Jane Russell led the Hollywood contingent
at McCarthy's party, and Oveta Culp Hobby was on the guest
list.

The physical appearance of our sets will be of supreme
importance in connection with the hotel which is shown,
just as it will be in connection with the Reata Ranch
house. To the precise extent that the art director follows
the arrangements and decor of the Shamrock Hotel, our
personification of Glenn McCarthy in the role of Jett
Rink will be made that much more certain. Edna Ferber
describes the hotel as being done in blue, whereas the
Shamrock is done in green. Other than that her disguise
is pretty thin. The extent of our disguise will depend
on the sets that are designed.

(D) LUZ BENEDICT, Bick's older sister, has no prototype
in real life. To an extent, she might be a composite of
Bob Kleberg's mother and a younger sister who was killed
in an automobile accident (in much the same way as Luz
dies in this story, except that it involved an automobile
and not a horse). On the whole, however, this seems to
be a fictional character and tends to help the position
that we are not personifying the Klebergs.

(E) UNCLE BAWLEY is represented by a real-life member of
the Kleberg dynasty. Instead of being an uncle of Bob
Kleberg he is a cousin, Caesar Kleberg, and instead of
running a northern section of the ranch he actually runs
the southernmost section of the King Ranch (the Norias
and Sauz divisions). Uncle Bawley of the novel and the
script is portrayed as a bachelor, living alone. The
description of Uncle Bawley's living arrangements which
is contained in the novel is identical with the description

TO: Eric Stacey

FROM: Tom Andre   7-25-55

James Dean was given a call for work (Interior of Truck -
Process) on Stage 5 upon his dismissal Friday night, July 22, by
both Rusty Meeks and Read Kilgore, second assistant directors,
for 8:30 AM makeup, to be ready at 9:00 AM. He was told he would
be through possibly by noon and arranged with Bob Hinkle (Texas
Talk Coach) to get him a pickup truck to move his residence from
1541 Sunset Playa Drive to a new residence (address unknown) in
Sherman Oaks. The truck was to be used after lunch on Saturday.

Saturday morning Dean was not in makeup at 8:30 and Rusty called
his (Dean's) message service - HOllywood 7-5191. Meeks was told
that Dean had been given a wake-up call at 8:00 and at 8:15. The
message service rang through to Dean who told Rusty Meeks he
would come right in. When he failed to show up numerous calls
were made from 9:30 to 10:15 to his home, with no one answering.

Dean's agent was asked to try and locate him and called in and
said that Dean was on his way in to the studio. That the "neigh-
bors" had seen Dean leave. Later the agent was again contacted
and went to Dean's Sunset Plaza address. Dean was not there. The
agent reported he also contacted Dean's new residence in the
valley and that Dean had not been seen there.

At twelve noon the company broke for lunch and it was decided to
leave the process equipment in case Dean showed up. Immediately
following the lunch break, since Dean had still not appeared, the
company moved to the Interior Reata Ranch House on Stage 4.

We obtained the make and license plates number of Dean's new car
and I, Tom Andre, asked Mr. Stevens if we should contact Blayney
Matthews in an effort to locate Dean. Mr. Stevens felt this
should not be done.

At 4:00 PM Rusty Meeks finally contacted Dean, who said that he
did not intend to come in to work. He said that when he got up in
the morning he was "too tired to work."

                                        TOM ANDRE

        T
        A
        /
        b
        c

From:Warner Bros. Studios
      Burbank, Calif.   9-1251

Ashton

Aug 55

      James Dean is reading all available books on Billy The Kid.
Dean, now portraying a Texan in "Giant," wants to do an authentic
film on the New York born bandit.

                              ***

Warner Bros.	25%
Pictures Presents	5%
George Stevens' Production	75%
G I A N T	100%
From the novel by	25%
Edna Ferber	50%

Starring

ELIZABETH TAYLOR	75%

CONTRACT: Must be
on scr. & in adv.
as shown, at per-
centage shown.

CONTRACT: Must star
or co-star on scr.
& in adv. No one
may be lgr. or
more prominent.

ROCK HUDSON	75%

CONTRACT: Must star or
co-star 2nd to Taylor on
scr. & in adv. no less
than 50% size of title
or word Giant, in event
Giant is lgr. than ti-
tle. No one may be lgr.
in lettering or promin-
ence. May fol. title if
co-stars do & "Starring"
precedes. If any artist
photo displayed, his will
be too in same rel. size
& imp. as co-stars. Need
not be in ads 4-col. in.
or less if no cast con-
tained therein.

JAMES DEAN	75%

CONTRACT: Must star or
co-star no less 3rd on
scr. & in adv., equal
size co-stars. No one
may be lgr. or more
prom. May fol. title if
co-stars do & "Starring"
precedes. Need not be in
ads 4-col.in. or less.

And Presenting
CARROLL BAKER	50%

CONTRACT: Must be
"Special Billed."

Also Starring

(CONTRACT: WITHERS must
be "Also Starring" on
scr. Size not specified
               WILLS must
be "Also Starring" on
scr. & in adv. Need not
be in adv. 4-col.in. or

JANE WITHERS	(
CHILL WILLS	(15% to 25%
MERCEDES McCAMBRIDGE	(
SAL MINEO	

McCAMBRIDGE must
be no less 4th "Also
Starring" on scr. & in
adv. Need not be in adv.
4-col.in. or less. Size not specified.

MINEO no adv.
obligation.

No adv. obligation

with

DENNIS HOPPER   10%

JUDITH EVELYN   10%

FAUL FIX   10%

Color by   25%
WarnerColor   50%

WRIT.CRED.must be in   Screen   10%
adv. in size & style   Fred Guiol   15%
ident.to Dir. or Prod.
(except where B.O.val.
or contract.oblig. to
either gives leeway.
Writers' names will be
in teaser, trailer &
group adv. if Dir. or
Prod. credited, unle
either has B.O. val.
Need not be in adv.
col. in. or less. See
Basic Agrmt. for c
exceptions.

CONTRACT: Must be
all adv. except a
8-col. in. or less
Size not specified.

Prod. & Dir. credits
need not be in group,
teaser, or ads less
than 8-col. in. See
Basic Agrmt. for
other exceptions.

WARNER BROS. PICTURES, INC.
BURBANK, CALIFORNIA

INTER-OFFICE COMMUNICATION   DATE ____ March 8, 1955

                                    SUBJECT ____ GIANT

MR. J. L. Warner
MR. George Stevens

Dear Jack:

          Eric Stacey informs me that you made inquiry of him if GIANT could
be made for the budget figure and that he was at a loss to give you information
on this matter short of a new script.   Unfortunately, this note came to me
too late before your departure to give you the following information:

          Original budget, plus all added costs, came to $2,912,500.   This
was $412,500 over our agreed-to $2,500,000 figure.   Since this date, no
commitment to an expenditure has been made without regard to necessary
reduction.   Following is the summary of expenditures so far:

          Three stars for cast, carried in budget at $350,000, have been pared
to $296,000 --
                                    Taylor - $175,000
                                    Hudson - 100,000
                                    Dean -   21,000

          Reduction here -- $54,000.
                                now OK'd and in work, called for an expenditure of
                                reduced   cost of $192,000. A redu

Presented by Warner Bros.   25%

FROM: WARNER BROS. STUDIOS   BURBANK, CALIF.   H09-1251   ASHTON

James Dean thinks every young actor should have a "Director's Notebook."
"A director's notebook," Dean explains, "is just an ordinary pad, but it has a very definite purpose in the acting profession.

"I use it to take notes on how a director works, how he uses lights, how he gets interesting and intricate camera angles, and just about every technique he employs in the shooting of a motion picture."

Dean first began using the notebook on "East of Eden". He says he took down more than 40 pages of notes on the directing technique of Elia Kazan.

"I hope to use the notes as research material and background data when I make that big move into the field of directing. I know it won't come for a long while, but I'm preparing," Dean says.

While filming Warner Bros.' "Rebel Without a Cause", Cinema-Scope-WarnerColor youth drama, Dean used up more than two notebooks observing the operation of Director Nicholas Ray.

"And when I went into George Stevens' production of "Giant" at Warners, I had another notebook," Dean explains.

"I hope to have a collection of notes on the technique of all of Hollywood's great motion picture directors."

James Dean kept his promise to George Stevens of no automobile racing during the filming of "Giant" at Warner Bros. Studios, but it didn't take him long to enter his first race after competing his role of Jett Rink a few days ago. Dean is entering the races at Salinas this weekend in the Porsche Spider he purchased last week.

FROM: WARNER BROS. STUDIOS   BURBANK, CALIF.   H09-1251 ASHTON

James Dean believes the old proverb, "a jack of all trades and a master of none," can be given a modern interpretation. In Dean's opinion a man who is a jack of all trades has a better chance of mastering the art of acting.

"An actor should know a little about many things," Dean says. "He must do more than project his own personality on the screen. He should represent a cross section of many phases of life. The best way to succeed in this is to learn as much as possible about people and their pursuits."

Dean, who is currently portraying ranch hand turned oil millionaire in "Giant", George Stevens' production for Warner Bros., concluded, "Any person stagnates if he does not add to his knowledge. I know I feel more alive when I am trying to master something new."

Dean has been practicing what he preaches in a variety of fields. His exploits on the automobile racing tracks were well publicised earlier this year. He won five trophies, though he had never raced before.

He gives intense concentration and dedication to any new interest. For his role of a Texas rancher in "Giant" he was determined to become expert at roping and horseback riding in order to get the feel of the man he was portraying. As a result he's now good enough to contemplate entering a rodeo or two as a fresh challenge.

On the cultural side, between scenes of "Giant" he has been concentrating on sculpting. He has already done busts of Edna Ferber, Elizabeth Taylor and one of himself.

During the past few years his restless curiosity has driven Dean to get acquainted with such varied pursuits as learning how to fight a bull, studying Aztec culture and playing the piano and the bongo drums. He also has learned to play tennis, to sail and has been studying several foreign languages.

Dean has a long list of things he wants to learn. "Some day I want to direct. A director must be a perfectionist and man of wide knowledge," he declared. "That is why I sometimes feel there are too few hours in the day to even begin to learn what I need to know."

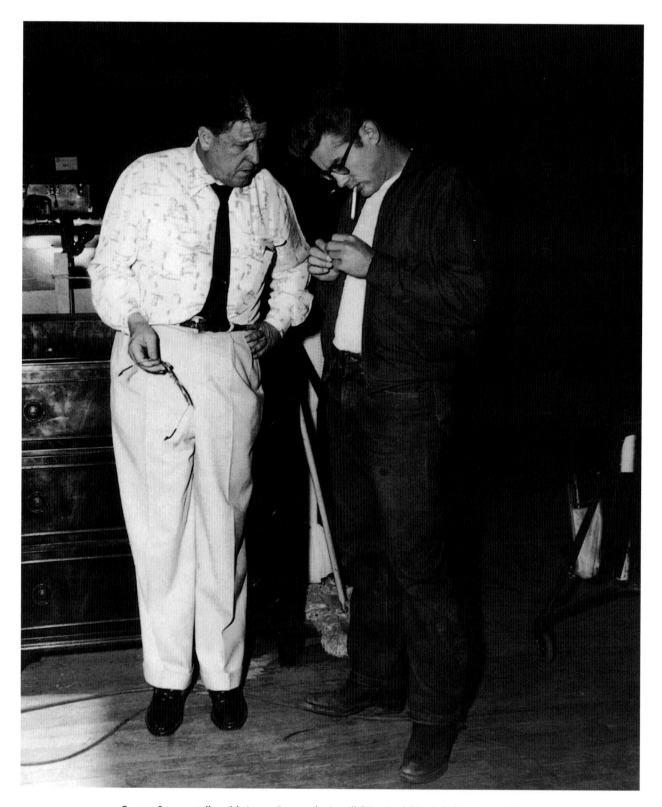

George Stevens talks with James Dean, who is still "Jim Stark" in *Rebel Without A Cause*.

"James Dean wanted to play Jett from the moment he heard that George Stevens … was planning to film *Giant*.

He began a subtle campaign to get the part weeks before the screenplay was even written."

WARNER BROS. PUBLICITY RELEASE TOM CARLILE: NOVEMBER, 1956

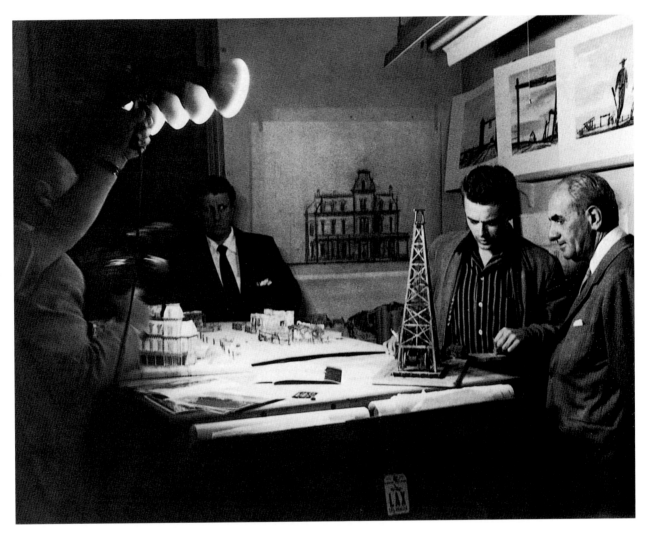

James Dean with Academy Award-winning art director Boris Leven concentrate on

Leven's model of the Little Reata oil derrick, which makes Jett Rink's fortune. Behind them

are some of Leven's design sketches for *Giant*.

A rehearsal reading of the script. James Dean is at the top right of the photograph. Clockwise from Dean:

Ray Whitley (Watts), Elsa Cardenas (Juana), Mary Ann Edwards (Mrs. Bale Clinch), George Dunne (Verne Decker),

Fran Bennett (Judy Benedict), unknown player, Alexander Scourby (Old Polo), Guy Teague (Harper), Chill Wills

(Uncle Bawley), Tina Menard (Lupe), Maurice Jara (Dr. Guerra), Carroll Baker (Luz Benedict II), Dennis Hopper

(Jordan Benedict III), Robert Nichols (Pinky Snythe), Sheb Wooley (Gabe Target), Victor Millan (Angel

Obregon),Charles Watts (Whiteside) and Bob Hinckle, Texas talk coach.

"Jimmy was Jimmy – maybe impossible to know really well. But wasn't that part of his fascination after all?"

CARROLL BAKER

Jett Rink watches Bick

Benedict's (Rock Hudson)

arrival at Reata with his new

bride Leslie (Elizabeth Taylor).

" ... muh car's broke."

James Dean makes a face

Up in the air planning the action, George Stevens tosses down a note

to the crew below while James Dean observes.

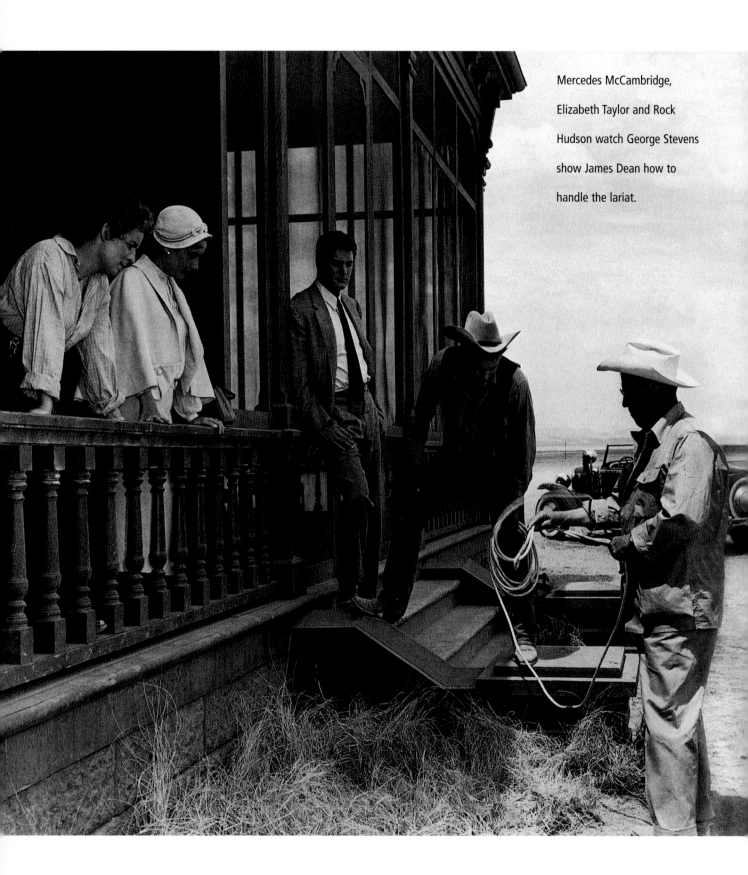

Mercedes McCambridge, Elizabeth Taylor and Rock Hudson watch George Stevens show James Dean how to handle the lariat.

"… he tried to make Jett a believable person by learning

the cowboy skills that made him a top ranch hand. Jimmy

learned to rope in a couple of weeks."

GEORGE STEVENS WARNER BROS. PUBLICITY RELEASE

TOM CARLILE NOVEMBER 1956

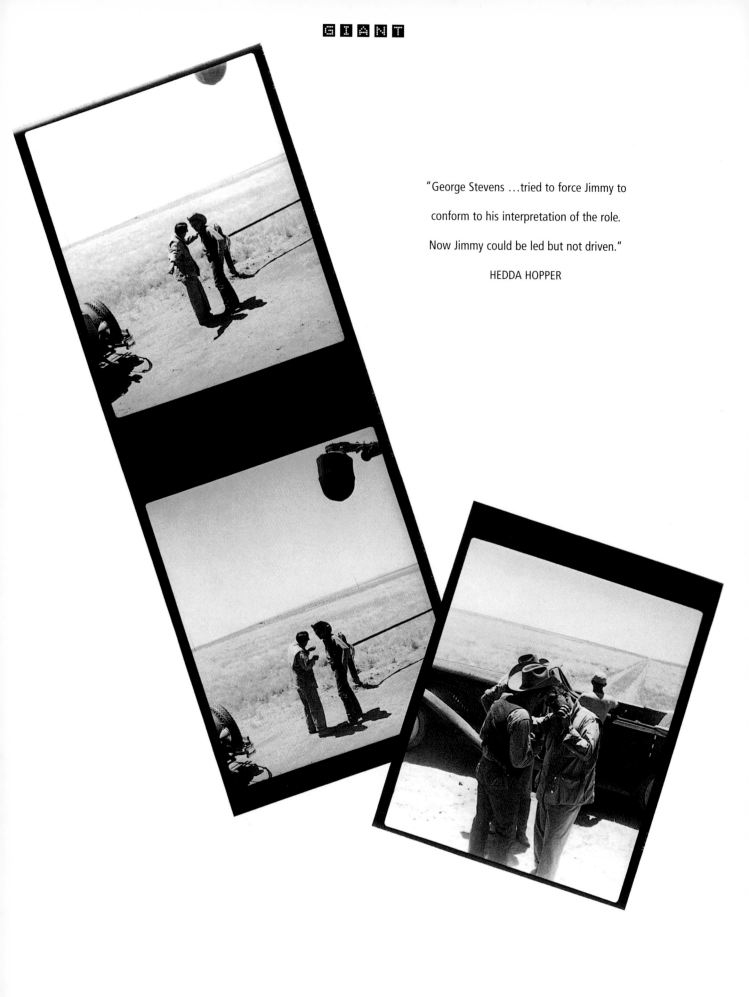

"George Stevens …tried to force Jimmy to
conform to his interpretation of the role.
Now Jimmy could be led but not driven."

HEDDA HOPPER

Walking down a road from nowhere – James Dean.

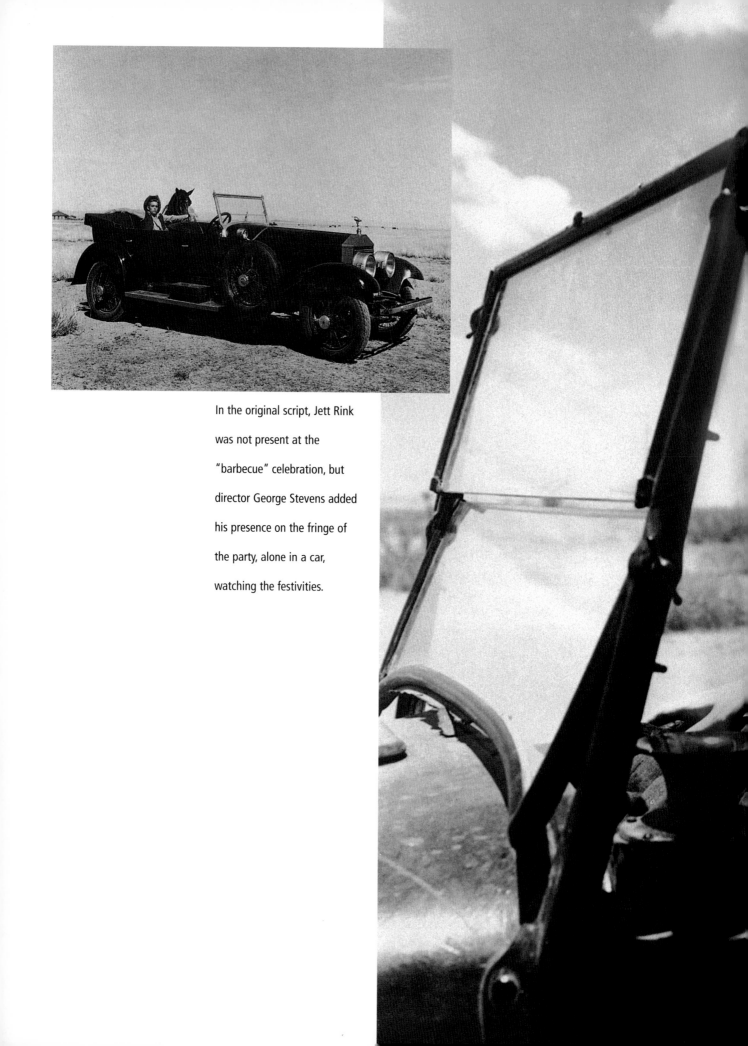

In the original script, Jett Rink was not present at the "barbecue" celebration, but director George Stevens added his presence on the fringe of the party, alone in a car, watching the festivities.

Mercedes McCambridge
and James Dean.

"He had the kind of
animal vitality that
cannot have escaped the
notice of the dry and
sequestered figure of
Bick's spinster sister, even
though she was almost
double his age."
JETT RINK: A PROFILE
WARNER BROS. STORY
DEPT. 1954

Jett Rink and Leslie Benedict – together on the Reata Ranch.

James Dean tells George
Stevens how he'd like to
play the scene.

… Abandoned …

On the Reata set at Warner Bros. in Burbank, Jett Rink practises rope tricks and waits for the reading of Luz's will.

learned to ride and rope
until he could twirl a
lariat as well as Will
Rogers." Hedda Hopper

Between scenes, James Dean

continues to perfect his rope tricks.

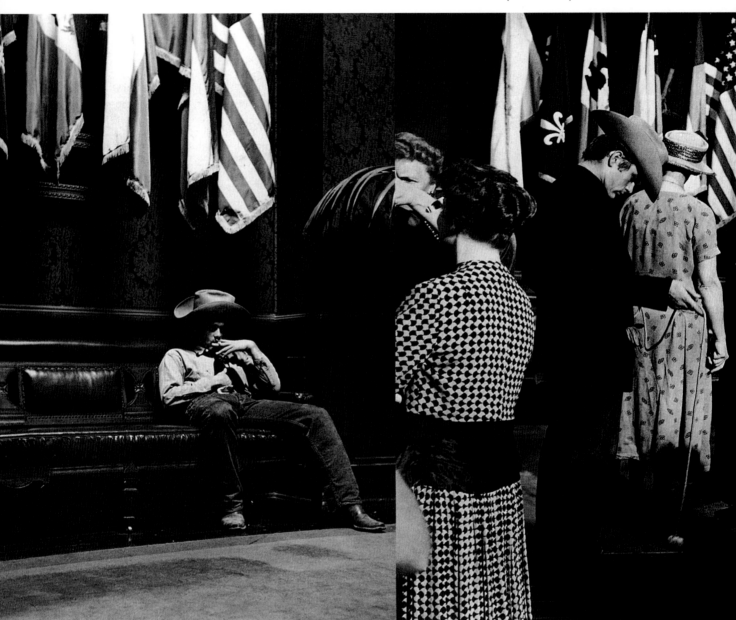

In preparation for a take, James

Dean becomes Napoleon

Bonaparte to *become* Jett Rink.

Jett Rink – alone in a crowd.

In the actual film, the shy Jett Rink

passes by Leslie Benedict and exits

without a word.

Following Luz's funeral, this meeting between Jett and Leslie does not occur in the finished film.

Jett Rink hangs his hat on a
post and prepares to walk
Little Reata, the piece of land
willed him by Luz Benedict.

EXTERIOR JETT RINK'S PLACE (DAY) 50M LONG SHOT.

Jett enters camera left – goes to windmill – climbs it –

looks – sits down.

CAMERA REPORT: *GIANT* SCENE 149

Finding the manmade shade a welcome relief from the hot Texas sun, James Dean and Henry

Ginsberg spend a few minutes together before the camera rolls again.

The main gate at Little Reata.

Right now, on Little Reata, water is the only thing that pours from the earth for Jett Rink and his dog.

Even under the hot Texas sun, the Hollywood production crew has to add more light in order to film Leslie Benedict's

arrival at Little Reata. An umbrella protects the camera from direct sunlight, but James Dean has to play the scene in

a heavy wool jacket, as if it was a chilly Texas morning.

Jett follows Leslie Benedict to his shack where he prepares tea for the only woman he'll ever really love.

Rehearsing one of the most famous photographs in movie history – "the crucifixion of James Dean".

While Leslie waits for her tea, Jett fortifies his courage.

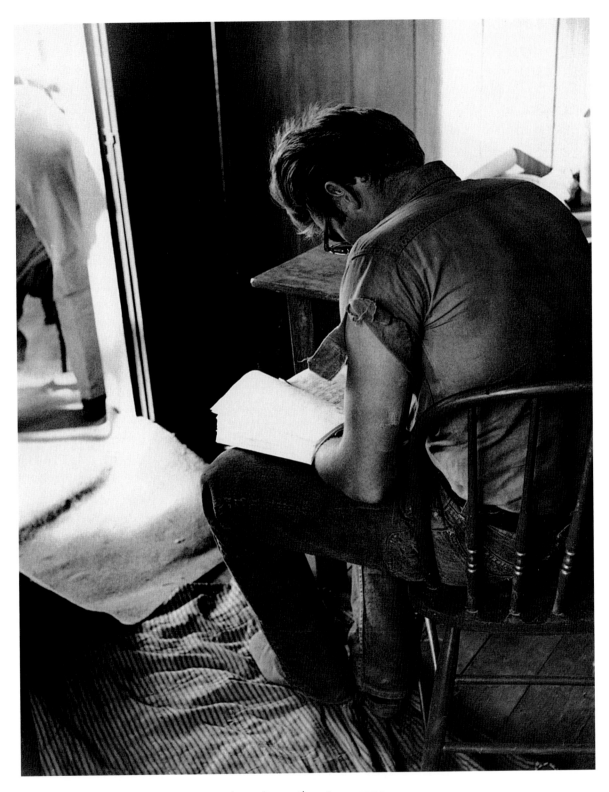

James Dean – the actor prepares.

In this sequence of photographs,
George Stevens shows two oil-
riggers how to carry the pipe while
James Dean watches closely.

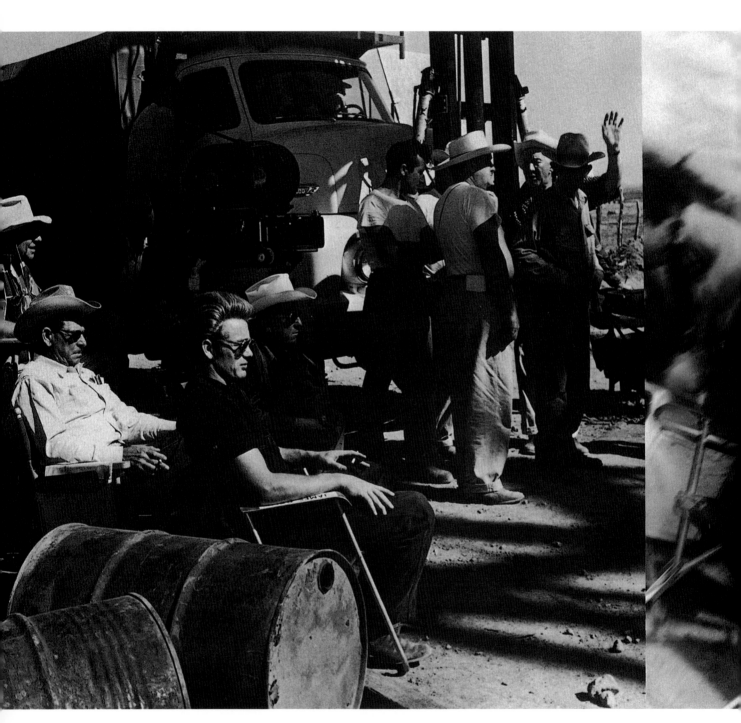

While the oil derrick is being readied – seated left to right:

Cinematographer Bill Mellor (wearing plaid shirt), 2nd Unit director Fred Guiol,

James Dean and George Stevens outside Marfa, Texas.

A gusher comes in and black gold reaches for the West Texas sky.

Before the next scene, James Dean applies his own "makeup" … not a pleasant experience.

Director George Stevens leans against a column and listens to a rehearsal of the fight between Bick Benedict and Jett Rink. In this sequence, Rock Hudson hits first … second … and third …

… but James Dean hits last.

"James Dean has been checking in at Warner Bros. Studios at 6.30 each morning for his

age make-up as Jett Rink in *Giant*, George Stevens' production of the Edna Ferber novel."

WARNER BROS. PUBLICITY RELEASE: TED ASHTON, AUGUST, 1955.

Ext. Jett's special built car day 2″ proc. (rear-screen projection) MCS (medium close shot)

Jett at wheel driving car through oil fields l-r. Has hat on – no glasses.

CAMERA REPORT: *GIANT*; SCENE 277.

"It was a great experience to work with Jimmy Dean. He was at once fully committed to the scene, entirely responsive to the other actor or actors, and yet a fierce competitor for first place."

CARROLL BAKER

EXIT

James Dean passes the camera on his way to the dais in the banquet room of the "Conquistador Hotel" as Guy Teague, Charles Watts and Ray Whitley obediently follow.

Bick Benedict squares off against a drunken
Jett Rink in the liquor storage room of the
"Conquistador Hotel".

hittin' – Jett. You want to
know something true?
You're all washed up."
BICK BENEDICT
GIANT

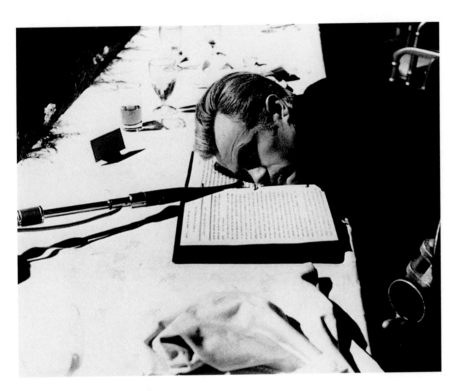

The camera catches Jett Rink

awakening from his stupor,

ready to give his speech.

In an empty banquet
room, alone on the dais,
framed between two
bottles, Jett Rink …

... begins his speech.

"Sight of the week. James Dean twirling himself around like a whirling dervish on the set of *Giant* at Warner Bros. He does it to get dizzy going into his tipsy scenes in the picture."
WARNER BROS. PUBLICITY
RELEASE TED ASHTON: 9/15/55

FORM 96 2500 SETS 5-54 SFPO4608

DAILY PRODUCTION AND PROGRESS REPORT

W-C WIDE SCREEN

Day __Saturday__   Date __10/1/55__

Name of Production	"GIANT"		No.	403	Name of Director
					GEORGE STEVENS

| Number of Days Alloted | 77 | Started Production | 5/19/55 | Days Elapsed Since Starting | 112 | Status of Schedule: 34 DAYS BEHIND SCH |

| Estimated Finish Date | 8/22/55 | Revised Finish Date (If Ahead or Behind) | | Name of Set | | Location | Finished? |

Company Called	8:00A	
Lng: Up.-Reh. 'til	11:58A	
Started Shooting	11:58A	
Lunch Called	12:32P	
Time Started	1:32P	
Dinner Called		
Time Started		
Time Finished	5:00P	

SCRIPT REPORT

No. of Scenes Original Script	473
No. of Scenes Previously Taken	374
No. of Scenes Taken Today	0
Total Scenes Taken to Date	374
Balance to Be Taken	99
No. of Added Scenes Taken	16 + 0 = 16

INT. REATA MAIN HALL & LIBRARY – 02

STAGE 4

CAST

S-Start W-Worked H-Held F-Finish R-Rehearse

		Time Started	Time Finished	Slate No.	No. of Takes	Time of Ok Takes
ELIZABETH TAYLOR ✱	W	8:15A	5:00P	1695	1	
ROCK HUDSON	W	6:30A	5:00P	1696	2	
CHILL WILLS	W	6:30A	5:00P	1697	4	
TINA MENARD	W	7:30A	5:45P	1698	1	
EARL HOLLIMAN	WF	11:00A	4:45P			
FRAN BENNETT	WF	11:00A	4:45P			
DENNIS HOPPER	WF	11:00A	4:45P			
RAMON RAMIREZ	W	2:00P	5:00P			
Photog. Dble. Wkly:						
TERESA KNIGHT	W	7:30A	5:00P			

STAFF

		Time Started	Time Finished
Supervisor	Ginsberg		
Director	Stevens		
Dial. Dir.	Hinkle		
Unit Mgr.	Andre		
1st Asst.	Rickards		
2nd Asst.	Kilgore		
Extra Asst.			
Script Clerk	Freedle		
Cutter	Hornbeck		
Art Dir.	Leven		
Tech. Adv'r.			
CAMERMAN			
Head	Mellor		
2nd	Phillips		
Asst.	Mathews		
	Faubion		
Still Man	McCarty		
PROP MEN			
Head	Moor		

AUTOS

Stand by—

In Scenes—

Added Scenes Taken

PRODUCTION 34 DAYS BEHIND SCHEDULE

REPORTED ON SET 11:45AM.

Remarks ✱ Note: ELIZABETH TAYLOR GRIEF STRICKEN

...iving later than time called, state rea...

NOTE: Kindly indi... If any artist delays director st...

Best Boy	
Grip	Harris / Clair
Makeup	6 Men
Hair Dr.	2 Women
Wdrbe.	Vallejo / Stutz

Today	
To Date	
ORCHESTRA (W) (R)	
Total	
Called	
Dismissed	
Setups Today	4
Pages Today	1
Pages to Date	161-7/8

5

EXTRAS	ANIMALS	LUNCHES	Script Scenes Taken
10 Babies	1 Lamb / 1 Calf		(Worked on Scenes 455 to end of script)
STAND-INS	ANIMAL HANDLERS	AUTOS	

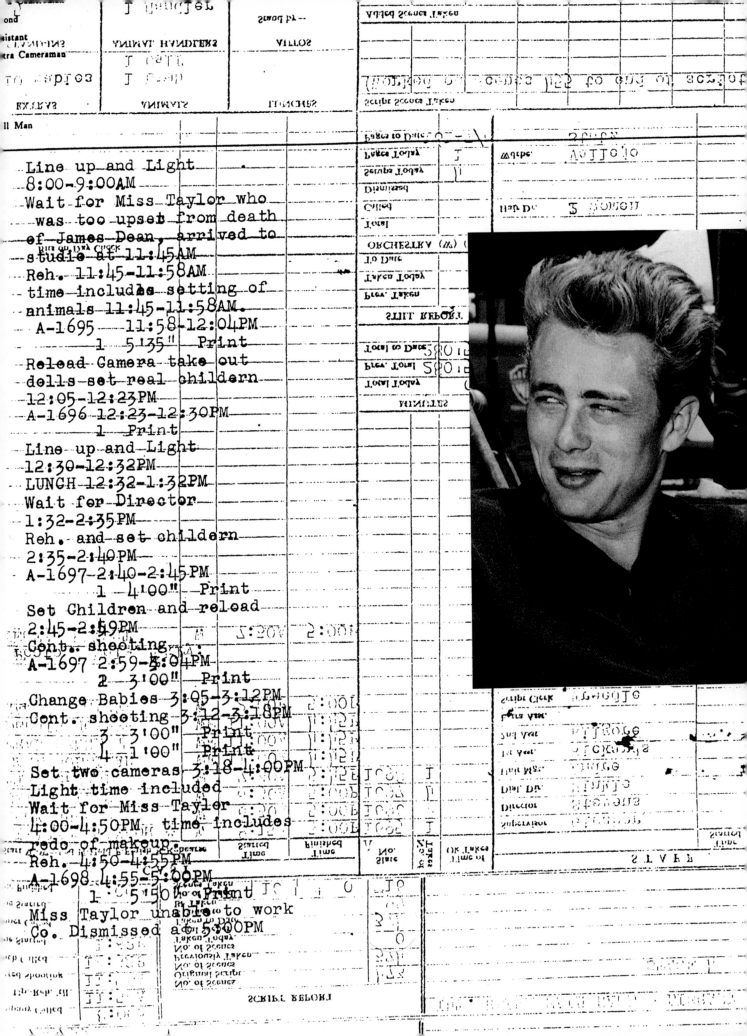

Line up and Light
8:00-9:00AM
Wait for Miss Taylor who
was too upset from death
of James Dean, arrived to
studio at 11:45AM
Reh. 11:45-11:58AM
time includes setting of
animals 11:45-11:58AM.
A-1695   11:58-12:04PM
        1 5:35" Print
Reload Camera take out
dolls-set real childern
12:05-12:23PM
A-1696 12:23-12:30PM
        1 Print
Line up and Light
12:30-12:32PM
LUNCH 12:32-1:32PM
Wait for Director
1:32-2:35PM
Reh. and set childern
2:35-2:40PM
A-1697-2:40-2:45PM
        1 4:00" Print
Set Children and reload
2:45-2:59PM
Cont. shooting
A-1697 2:59-3:04PM
        2 3:00" Print
Change Babies 3:05-3:12PM
Cont. shooting 3:12-3:18PM
        3 3:00" Print
        4 1:00" Print
Set two cameras 3:18-4:00PM
Light time included
Wait for Miss Taylor
4:00-4:50PM time includes
redo of makeup
Reh. 4:50-4:55PM
A-1698 4:55-5:00PM
        1 5:50" Print
Miss Taylor unable to work
Co. Dismissed at 5:00PM

In order to keep their star happy and occupied, Warner Bros. and Elia Kazan, Nick Ray and George Stevens allowed James Dean to do something only a union studio photographer was allowed to do – shoot publicity photos during the making of *East of Eden*, *Rebel Without a Cause* and *Giant*.

The studio processed the film and the negatives and prints lingered behind with all the others that the Publicity Photo Deaprtment deemed unnecessary for the general promotion of the movies. They too ended up in the WB Archives at USC, mixed in with all the other negs and prints from the three films.

But something about these photos made them stand out. At first, it was their utterly unprofessional quality … odd angles often coupled with murky lighting. "What the hell are these?" was out first thought when Keith and I started our search through the material.

Then the realization hit. These were the photos Dean was allowed to take of his fellow actors – his directors – his girlfriend. Here is Pier Angeli – too beautiful for words – at her makeup table for *The Silver Chalice*. There is Raymond Massey on his 'death bed' as Adam Trask … and Barbara Baxley as his nurse … and there's Julie Harris vamping for the camera … and Elia Kazan mugging … and Nick Ray glowering. Natalie Wood is there, too … and even some unnamed microphone boom men … all seen through the eye of James Dean. Here, then, is JAMES DEAN – BEHIND THE CAMERA.

BEHIND·THE·CAMERA

Rebel Without a Cause, 1955

Giant, 1955

Pier Angeli, 1954

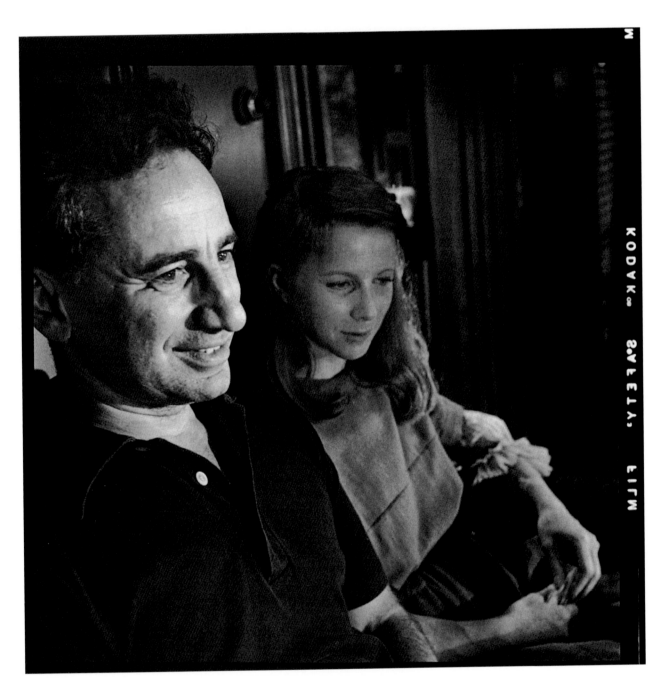

Elia Kazan and Julie Harris, 1954

Julie Harris, 1954

Barbara Baxley, 1954

Raymond Massey, 1954

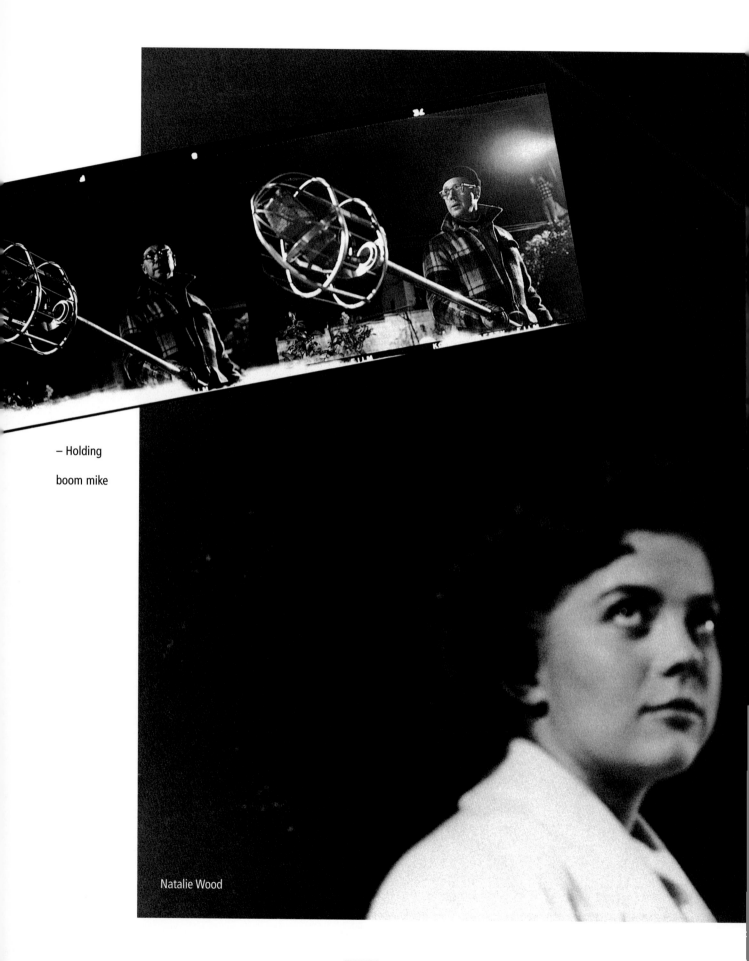

– Holding

boom mike

Natalie Wood

Director Nick

Ray, 1955

Floyd McCarty's hotel

Room. Marfa, Texas, 1955.

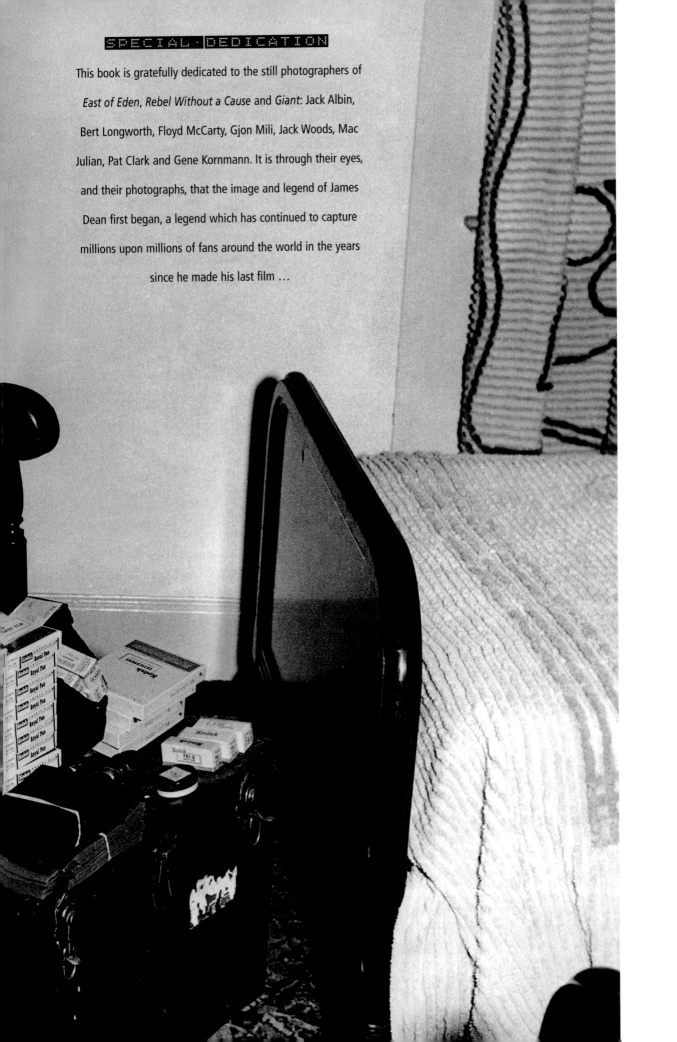

SPECIAL · DEDICATION

This book is gratefully dedicated to the still photographers of *East of Eden*, *Rebel Without a Cause* and *Giant*: Jack Albin, Bert Longworth, Floyd McCarty, Gjon Mili, Jack Woods, Mac Julian, Pat Clark and Gene Kornmann. It is through their eyes, and their photographs, that the image and legend of James Dean first began, a legend which has continued to capture millions upon millions of fans around the world in the years since he made his last film …

EPILOGUE

"On Friday, September 30, around six o'clock, Elizabeth, Rock and I and a small group were watching the rushes. George Stevens was behind us at his desk by the controls. The projection room was dark. The phone rang. The soundtrack screamed to a halt. The picture froze, The lights shot up. We turned and looked at George. The phone dangled in his hand. He was white and motionless. Death was present in that room. Slowly and with great effort, his voice coming from a long and distant tunnel, George said, "There's been a car crash. Jimmy Dean has been killed." I went numb.

Oct. 5, 1955

Miss Hedda Hopper
6331 Hollywood Blvd.
Hollywood, Calif.

Dear Miss Hopper:

I'm very grateful to you for the beautiful eulogy in your column about Jimmy Dean.

I was Mr. Kazan's secretary on EAST OF EDEN and knew (and understood) Jimmy from that moment on. You're right – this boy had a lot of love to give, but perhaps was afraid of being rejected, like so many sensitive people. The birthday scene in EAST OF EDEN, which was almost unbearable to watch, must have been easy for Jimmy to do. I'll always be haunted by that terrible sob that seemed to come from his soul.

It's too bad that people judge that first deceiving, unimportant layer instead of trying to understand sensitive people – there's a lot of good stuff underneath! Toothy, insincere smiles and glad hands are a dime a dozen.

Thank you again – very much.

Sincerely,

Rhea Burakoff

1830 N. Cherokee
Hollywood 28, Calif.

Thursday October 6

Dear John –

The passing of James Dean was indeed very tragic. He had a magnificent career ahead of him. He had completed his role in our picture two weeks before the accident, hence there was nothing further that he was required to do for us. He gave a great performance in GIANT and his ageing from the early 20's to about 50 years is most realistic and convincing. The consensus of opinion personality and may develop into something of a legend. Considering that he was a character actor, the feeling is that his appearance in films will not be affected at all, if anything there may be greater anxiety on the part of the public to see him. It must be borne in mind that he only made one picture thus far released which, as you know, is EAST OF EDEN, and he reached stardom overnight. Warners have another picture unreleased-REBEL WITHOUT A CAUSE. Although I have not seen it, I am told that it is only fair, however, his performance is most outstanding. This picture will be released sometime in November and this may be a guide somewhat to public reaction. Our picture GIANT is naturally protected by other star personalities and we probably will not release our picture for another year. Of course the thinking I am giving you is of today and it is difficult to say what will happen a year hence.

I am leaving here in the morning for Fairmont, Indiana to attend Dean's funeral services and I will return to the coast on Sunday.

My love and best to you,

Dad

From Wed. Oct. 5, 1955 Column

"I'm still reeling from the sudden death of Jimmy Dean, one of the greatest acting talents I've ever known. He was a tragic figure. So few understood him. He was reaching out for love and understanding, but got so little. His greatest ambition was to play Hamlet on Broadway. Said he, "It should only be done by a young man." The thing that he loved most was the thing that killed him – his racing car. He carried with him in death the St. Christopher medal Pier Angeli gave him while he was making "EAST OF EDEN." He was like quicksilver. He had a sure instinct for drama. He was like the parched earth longing for the rain. Only a few days ago a friend of mine met him in a pet hospital. He had brought a kitten for innoculation and the loving care he was giving it was beautiful to look upon. It will be a long time before we see his like again. I loved the boy and always will."

ACKNOWLEDGEMENTS

To the following people, without whose help, inspiration and support, this book would not exist …
Mr. Bernard Kurman: Rights Unlimited Agency

Warner Bros. Inc.: Luana Chambers, Dan Romanelli, Patricia Brown, Marshall Silverman, Judy Singer, Jeremy Williams, John Schulman, Betty Buckley, Irene Slade, Paula Reno, Jackie Kelly, Wendy Abbott.

USC: Herbert Farmer, Anne Schlosser, Ned Constock, Victoria Steele, Carolyn Harrison, Robert Knutson.

UCLA: Brigitte Kueppers, Raymond Soto, David Zeidberg, James Davis.

Producers Photo Lab: Knight Harris, Clark Harris, Lee Lawrence, Scott Libolt, Craig Bright, Herayr Nazarian.

Margaret Herrick Library, Academy of Motion Picture Arts & Sciences: Sam Gill, Stacey Endres, Howard Prouty, Linda Mehr.

Birch Lane Press: Hillel Black, Sandy Richardson, Gail Kinn, Steven Schragis, Bruce Bender, Steven Brower, Jessica Black, Ben Petrone, Fern Edison.

Book Castle of Burbank, California: Paul Hunt, Steve Edrington.

The entire staff of Movie World in Burbank, California.

Dennis Hopper, John Waxman, Sid Avery, Bill Zavatsky, Faith McNulty, Douglas M. Spruance, James Erlandson, Natasha Arnoldi, Robin Berg, the Henry Ginsberg Family.

To Wyatt and Jane Adams and Harry and Rose Burns who gave us the money for the tickets and put the boxes of popcorn into our hands … our parents, who hooked us on the movies forever.

And especially to Char Adams and Joan Perkal for their love and support through the years it has taken this book to reach this moment and for allowing us and the book to spill over into the living rooms of their lives.

ACKNOWLEDGEMENTS FOR · BOOK · QUOTES

Grateful acknowledgment is given to the following publishers for their permission to reprint the excerpts included in this book.

Backus, Jim. *Rocks On the Roof*. New York: G. P. Putnma Sons, 1958

Baker, Carroll. *Baby Doll — An Autobiography*. New York: Arbor House, 1983

Chekmayan, Ara. *Forever James Dean*. A Chelsea Communications Production, 1988

Hopper, Hedda. *The Whole Truth and Nothing But*. New York: Doubleday, 1963

Kazan, Elia. *A Life*. New York: Alfred A Knopf, 1988

Massey Raymond. *A Hundred Different Lives*. Boston: Little, Brown and Company, 1979

McCambridge, Mercedes. *The Quality of Mercy*. New York: Times Books, 1981

Sheinwald, Patricia Fox. *Too Young to Die*. Baltimore: Ottenheimer Publishing, Inc., 1979

EAST OF EDEN

Warner Bros. (Released March 1955)

Produced and directed by Elia Kazan; Screenplay by Paul Osborn; Based on the novel by John Steinbeck; Cinematography, Ted McCord; Art direction, James Basevi and Malcolm Bert, Musical direction, Leonard Rosenman; Editor, Owen Marks. CinemaScope and WarnerColor. 155 minutes

James Dean (Cal Trask); Julie Harris (Abra); Raymond Massey (Adam Trask); Burl Ives (Sam); Jo Van Fleet (Kate); Richard Davalos (Aron Trask); Albert Dekker (Will); Lois Smith (Anne); Harold Gordon (Mr. Albrecht); Richard Garrick (Dr. Edwards); Timothy Carey (Joe); Nick Dennis (Rantini); Lonnie Chapman (Roy); Barbara Baxley (Nurse); Bette Treadville (Madame); Tex Mooney (Bartender); Harry Cording (Bartender); Loretta Rush (Card Dealer); Bill Phillips (Coalman);Mario Siletti (Piscora); Jonathan Piscora's Son); Jack Carr, Effie Laird, Wheaton Chambers, Ed Clark, Al Ferguson, Franklyn Farnum, Rose Plummer (Carnival People); John George (Photographer); Earle Hodgins (Shooting Gallery Attendatnt); C. Ramsey Hill (English Officer); Edward McNally (Solider)

(James Dean was nominated for an Academy Award as Best Actor)

REBEL WITHOUT A CAUSE

Warner Bros. (Released October 1955)

Produced by David Weisbart; Directed by Nicholas Ray; Screenplay by Stewart Stern; Based on Irving Shulman's adaptation of a story by Nicholas Ray; Cinematography, Ernest Haller; Art direction, Malcolm Bert; Costumes, Moss Mabry; Musical direction, Leonard Rosenman; Editor, William Ziegler.
CinemaScope and WarnerColor. 111 minutes.

James Dean (Jim); Natalie Wood (Judy); Sal Mineo (Plato); Jim Backus (Jim's Father); Ann Doran (Jim's Mother); Corey Allen (Buzz); William Hopper (Judy's Mother); Virginia Brissac (Jim's Grandma); Nick Adams (Moose); Jack Simmons (Cookie); Dennis Hopper (Goon); Marietta Canty (Plato's Maid); Jack Grinnage (Chick); Beverly Long (Helen); Steffi Sidney (Mil); Frank Mazzola (Crunch); Tom Bernard (Harry); Clifford

Morris (Cliff); Ian Wolfe (Lecturer); Edward Platt (Ray); Robery Foulk (Gene); Jimmy Baird (Beau); Dick Wessel (Guide); Nelson Leigh (Sergeant); Dorothy Abbott (Nurse); Louise Lane (Woman Officer); House Peters (Officer); Gus Schilling (Attendant); Bruce Noonan (Monitor); Almira Sessions (Old Lady Teacher); Peter Miller (Hoodlum); Paul Bryar (Desk Sergeant); Paul Birch (Police Chief); Rober B. Williams (Moose's Father); David McMahon (Crunch's Father)

GIANT

Warner Bros. (Released October 1956)

Produced by George Stevens and Henry Ginsberg; Directed by George Stevens; Screenplay by Fred Guiol and Ivan Moffat; Based on the novel by Edna Ferber; Cinematography, William C. Mellor; Production designer, Boris Leven; Costumes, Marjorie Best and Moss Mabry; Musical score, Dimitri Tiomkin; Song "There's Never Been Anyone Else But You" by Dimitro Tiomkin and Paul Francis Webster; Editor, William Hornbeck. WarnerColor, 198 minutes.

Elizabeth Taylor (Leslie Lynnton Benedict); Rock Hudson (Bick Benedict); James Dean (Jett Rink); Carroll Baker (Luz Benedict II); Jane Withers (Vashti Snythe); Chill wills (Uncle Bawley); Mercedes McCambridge (Luz Benedict); Sal Mineo (Sal Mineo (Angel Obregon III); Dennis Hopper (Jordan Benedict III); Judith Evelyn (Mrs. Horace Lynnton); Paul Fix (Dr. Horace Lynnton); Rodney Taylor (Sir David Karfrey); Earl Holliman (Bob Dace); Robert Nichols (Pinky Snythe); Alexander Scourby (Old Polo); Fran Bennett (Judy Benedict); Charles watts (Whiteside); Elsa Cardenas (Juana); Carolyn Craig (Lacey Lynnton); Monte Hale (Bale Clinch); Mary Ann Edwards (Adarene Clinch); Sheb Wooley (Gabe Target); Victor Millan (Angel Obregon I); Mikcey Simpson (Sarge); Pilar del Rey (Mrs. Obregon); Maurice Jara (Dr. Guerra); Noreen Nash (Lona Lane); Napoleon Whiting (Swazey); Tina Menard (Lupe); Ray Whitley (Watts); Felipe Turich (Gomez); Francisco Villalobos (Mexican Priest); Ana Maria Majalca (Petra); Guy Teague (Harper); Nativadid Vacio (Eusebio); Max Terhine (Dr. Walker); Ray Bennett (Dr. Borneholm); Barbara Barrie (Mary Lou Decker); George Dunne (Verne Decker); Slim Talbot (Clay Hodgins); Tex Driscoll (Clay Hodgins, Sr.); Juney Ellis (Essie Lou Hodgins)

(James Dean was nominated for an Academy Award as Best Actor)